Selections from the
Lewis Carroll Collection
of Victoria J. Sewell

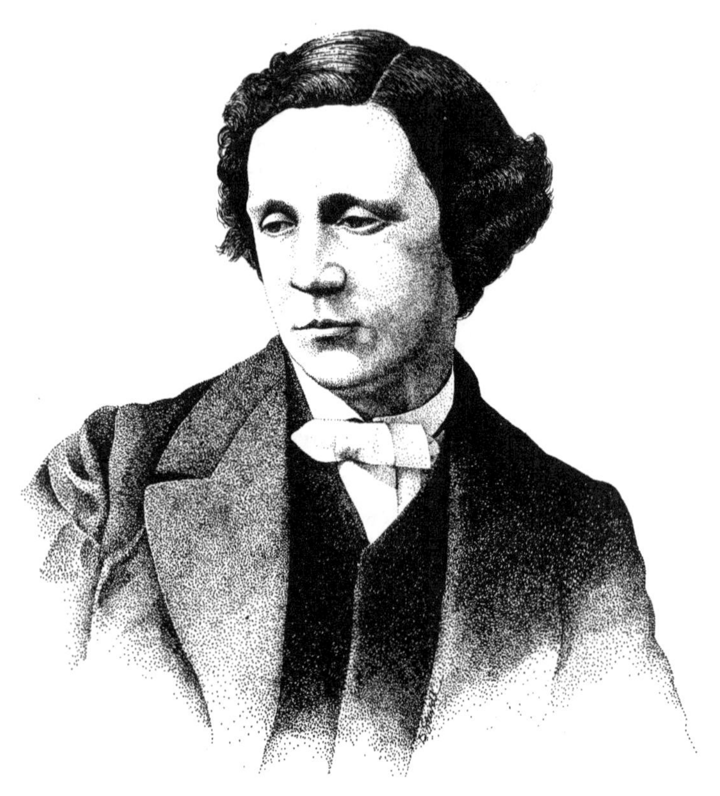

LEWIS CARROLL

Selections from the Lewis Carroll Collection of Victoria J. Sewell

A Sesquicentennial Celebration
of the First Publication of
Alice's Adventures in Wonderland

COMPILED AND ANNOTATED BY

BYRON W. SEWELL

PREFACE BY

EDWARD WAKELING

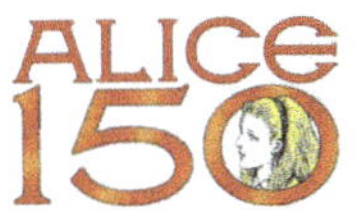

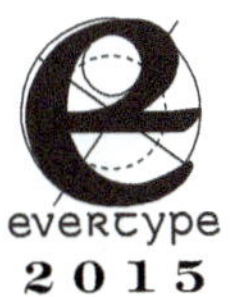

THE HUNTINGTON MUSEUM OF ART
HUNTINGTON, WEST VIRGINIA
MAY 30 TO SEPTEMBER 9, 2015

evertype
2015

Published by Evertype, 73 Woodgrove, Ballyfin Road, Portlaoise, Co. Laois, Ireland. *www.evertype.com*.

Contents

Preface *VII*

Foreword: The 150th Anniversary *VIII*

Lewis Carroll and the Arts *XIII*

Down the Rabbit-Hole *XV*

Collecting Lewis Carroll *XIX*

Catalogue of the Exhibition *1*

Jett Jackson's *Stuck in Wonderland* *91*

Alice150 Celebrations and Exhibitions *95*

The Lewis Carroll Society
of North America *98*

Acknowledgements *99*

Preface

HARIETTE CYRUS
DIRECTOR OF THE HUNTINGTON MUSEUM OF ART

Back in the summer of 2012, when Victoria Sewell's grand-children were attending Summer Camp here at the Huntington Museum of Art, Victoria spoke with our curator, Jenine Culligan, about the *Alice* collection maintained by herself and her husband Byron Sewell. She told me that 2015 was the 150th anniversary of the publication of *Alice's Adventures in Wonderland* and that they would be willing to share their collection with the Museum.

So, "Alice150: Selections from the Lewis Carroll Collection of Victoria J. Sewell" was born. It was such a nice surprise to find out about their collection and for the Museum to become a part of the celebration of a book with which everyone is familiar.

The Huntington Museum of Art is very excited to be a part of the 150th anniversary of the publication of Lewis Carroll's *Alice* by sharing the Sewell's collection with *Alice* fans all over the Tri-State region.

Foreword:
The 150th Anniversary

EDWARD WAKELING
EDITOR OF *LEWIS CARROLL'S DIARIES*

The genesis of *Alice's Adventures in Wonderland* owes much to Oxford University in England. The lecturer in mathematics at Christ Church, Charles Lutwidge Dodgson, better known to the world as Lewis Carroll, took the three daughters of the Dean, Lorina, Alice, and Edith Liddell, on a much anticipated river-trip to Godstow on the 4th of July 1862, accompanied by Robinson Duckworth from University College. The trip had been delayed by rain the previous day. However, the following afternoon the sun shone, and the children enjoyed the singing of Duckworth and the improvised story-telling of Dodgson as the boat was rowed up river. On their return to Christ Church that evening, Alice Liddell implored Dodgson to write out the fantastical story he had invented. He said he "would try."

This was quite an undertaking as Dodgson had used nothing more than his creative imagination – no plan and no notes to help him reconstruct the story, just a good memory. He spent the following day, on a railway journey to London, jotting down as many of the ideas in the story that he could remember, but nothing happened for some months afterwards. It is likely that an impatient Alice reminded Dodgson of his promise during the Michaelmas term (in the Fall) because he notes in his diary that he began writing out the text on November 13, 1862. Dodgson sat in his room in Tom 7:3 (now the Junior Common Room) and completed the manuscript, written out in a careful non-cursive hand to look like the printed page, on the 10th of February 1863. But he left spaces for the illustrations, a more daunting task since Dodgson was not a trained artist.

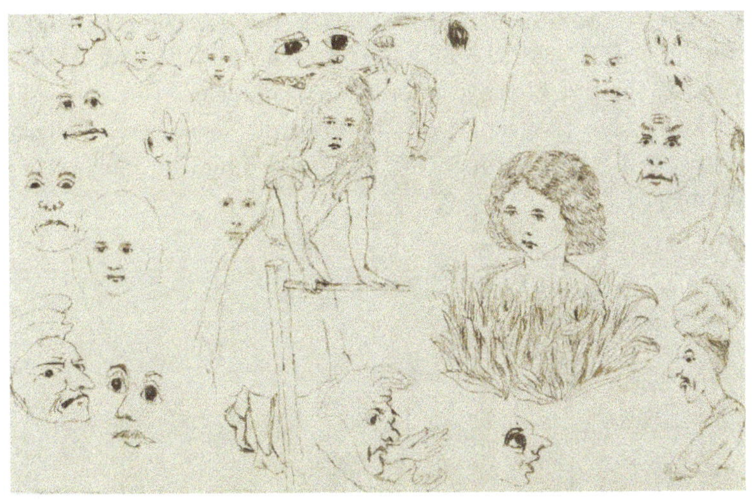

The Library at Christ Church contains some unique manuscripts that show how Dodgson practised his drawings before inserting them into the manuscript, a task that took him many months. We know that Dodgson consulted books on natural history from the Library to help with accuracy. There are drawings of guinea pigs, a lizard, a flamingo, rabbits, a mole, a puppy, various fish, a sea-horse, a mouse, and a caterpillar. Two imaginary creatures, a gryphon and a mock-turtle are beautifully drawn, but the initials "W.L.D." indicate that these were done by his brother, Wilfred Longley Dodgson, who had been an undergraduate at Christ Church (1856–60). There are various drawings of the fictional Alice in various positions; standing, seated, drawing back a curtain, head squashed down to her toes (part of the story), head resting on her arm, profiles of her head, swimming, holding a flamingo under her arm, and so on. Strangely, among the preliminary drawings are the heads of elves, goblins and other mythical creatures that do not appear in the final version of the story. These were clearly a feature of some tales told to the Liddell children during the boat-trip, but Dodgson chose not to include them in the final version of the story.

Once completed, the manuscript pages, now with their illustrations, were stitched together and bound in green leather. Almost two and a half years after the river-trip, Dodgson presented Alice with the manuscript of *Alice's Adventures Under Ground* (the title of the original story) as an early Christmas gift for 1864 (she received it on the 26th of November). Dodgson inscribed it "A Christmas Gift to a Dear Child in Memory of a Summer Day."

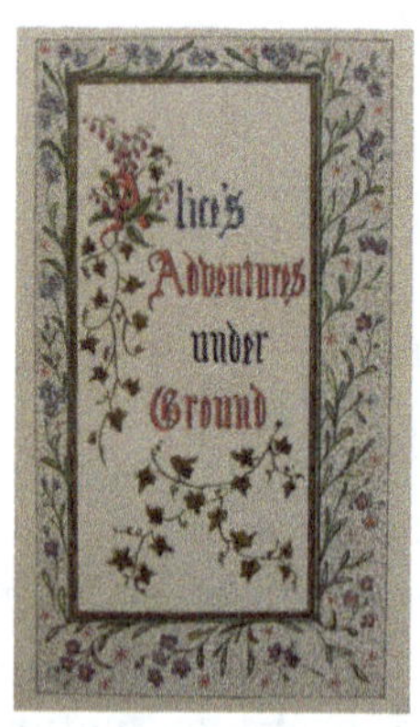

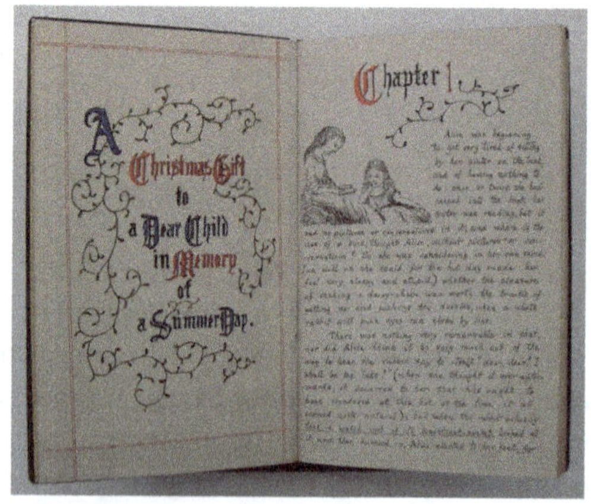

But this is not the end of the story. During the preparation of the manuscript a number of Dodgson's friends saw the pages and had a chance to read them. He was strongly encouraged to publish the book. So before the manuscript was presented to Alice Liddell, he set in motion the process of getting the story prepared for publication. He originally intended to publish the book with his own illustrations, and he arranged for the book to be printed at the Clarendon Press at his own expense. They provided him with woodblocks and pencils so that he could copy his drawings from the manuscript onto blocks for the engraver. The result was not a success. Following advice from artistic friends, he decided to obtain the services of a professional illustrator. Typically for Dodgson, he aimed for the best.

Dodgson was already acquainted with the dramatist and civil servant, Tom Taylor, who was a regular contributor to *Punch*. Dodgson wrote to him on the 20th of December 1863 asking for an introduction to the "number one" illustrator in *Punch*, John Tenniel. The request was successful. Dodgson called on Tenniel for the first time on the 25th of January 1864 and noted in his diary that Tenniel seemed willing to undertake the pictures but wanted to see the book before deciding. Tenniel took his time to consider the commission and finally wrote to Dodgson at the beginning of April 1864 consenting to draw the pictures for *Alice's Adventures*.

Dodgson was still not clear about a title for the published book, so he wrote to Tom Taylor to seek his advice. Dodgson had various titles in mind including "Alice's hour in Elf-Land," "Alice among the Goblins," and "Alice's Adventures in Wonderland." The latter was chosen, but from this we can see that elves and goblins formed a part of the intended book as Dodgson rewrote the story of *Under Ground* (12,790 words) into the much expanded published version of *Wonderland* (27,240 words). New episodes were included such as "Pig and Pepper" (chapter 6) and "A Mad Tea-Party" (chapter 7), neither of which contained elves or goblins.

Dodgson began to prepare for the publication by designing the title page, and a number of drafts survive in the Library. The first, hand-written, spells Tenniel's name incorrectly, and announces "twenty-four" illustrations. Tenniel, already with a high reputation as the chief illustrator for *Punch,* did not come cheap. But Dodgson realized that Tenniel's work would give his book a much better chance of success.

The Clarendon Press produced some trial title pages, using various sizes of type for the title, which was now *Alice's Adventures in Wonderland*, with illustrations by Tenniel, and the date given as 1864. Dodgson eventually settled for 42 illustrations, but the book did not come out until 1865. In the meantime, Dodgson met Tenniel frequently in London to discuss the illustrations as the book evolved from *Under Ground* to *Wonderland*.

A plan for the 42 illustrations was constructed, which survives in the Library, and this outlines the number of illustrations for each chapter, the subject, and the height and width of the picture required. The document is in Dodgson's hand, and he also indicated whether the picture was to be central on a page or "let in" from either the right or left of the page. He also added page numbers as the book was set in type.

Dodgson was keen to have the book ready for the third anniversary of that fateful boat-trip so that he could present Alice Liddell with a specially bound copy on the 4th of July 1865. The book was set in type and 2,000 copies printed by the Clarendon Press. However, in their haste to get the book ready by Dodgson's deadline, the process was unduly hurried resulting in some minor variation in print intensity and some "bleeding through" of the text onto the verso pages. In a few cases, the print from the underside of a page affected Tenniel's illustrations. The overall effect is hardly of major concern, yet Tenniel, a man with a reputation at stake, was unhappy with the result. Dodgson had already given away some copies of the first edition, bound up for presentation purposes, which he hastily tried to retrieve.

Dodgson ordered a reprint on the 2nd of August, but this time it was typeset by Richard Clay in London. Dodgson received a copy of the new impression of *Alice* on the 28th of November 1865, which, to Dodgson's relief, was fully approved of by Tenniel. The first published edition of *Alice's Adventures in Wonderland* was available for the Christmas market in December 1865, but all copies bear the date 1866 on the title page.

2015 sees the 150th anniversary of the first publication of *Alice*, and the occasion will be marked by events, television programmes, books, and exhibitions around the globe.

Lewis Carroll and the Arts

BYRON W. SEWELL

*C*harles Lutwidge Dodgson, better known today as Lewis Carroll, was keenly interested in the visual and performance arts for his entire life. As a child and young man he illustrated stories he wrote for the entertainment of his brothers and sisters in home magazines with excellent comic effect. Likewise, he initially illustrated the original manuscript for what ultimately became *Alice's Adventures Under Ground*, the precursor to *Alice's Adventures in Wonderland*. Even though an early friend assured him that he lacked the necessary drawing skills to effectively illustrate *Alice* for publication (advice that led him to seek the services of *Punch's* chief cartoonist, John Tenniel) his own illustrations were eventually published. In late Victorian and modern times Carroll's own illustrations have been widely admired and acclaimed.

One of Dodgson's primary early contributions to the visual arts was his pioneering photography. Original prints of his early photographs can today command five-figure sums at auction and are considered to be some of the best examples of Victorian children ever taken. Dodgson possessed a gifted eye and intellect for composition, form and content, essential ingredients for all accomplished visual artists.

Dodgson was a keen and enthusiastic supporter of the Victorian theatre, often taking his child-friends to London performances. He became close friends of many of the most famous Victorian actors and actresses, including Ellen Terry and members of her family. His agreement to allow H. Savile Clarke to produce *Alice* for the Victorian stage led to decades of performances and revivals. Some of the actors and actresses that became late-Victorian and Edwardian luminaries got their stage breaks in these performances.

Dodgson's close circle of friends included many of the most famous Victorian artists, including members of the Pre-Raphaelite Brotherhood, including William Holman Hunt, John Everett Millais and Dante Gabriel Rossetti. Dodgson attended the famous juried London art shows and actually owned several Pre-Raphaelite paintings.

Due to the enormous success of Carroll's *Alice* books, he has provided a platform and inspiration for numerous illustrators and artists around the world to illustrate thousands of different illustrated editions, and in modern times has been the inspiration for hundreds of plays and movies, all of which haves been of enormous financial benefit to countless artists, performers, designers, and producers. It is not an overstatement to say that Carroll's influence has been a major contributor to Popular Culture.

Down the Rabbit-Hole

VICTORIA J. SEWELL

My first encounter with *Alice in Wonderland* was at a Union Carbide Hunting and Fishing Club meeting in my hometown of South Charleston, WV when I was six years old. To entertain the children during the meeting the members showed the 1951 Disney cartoon version of *Alice* on a large screen. During the scene when Alice falls down the rabbit-hole I ran, terrified, from the room to find my father. After finding him in a "forest" of legs in dress pants, I convinced him, in-between sobs, that it was not something I wanted to see. To my young mind, this was a scary film and not suitable for children. I suppose you could say I was "traumatized" by the Disney movie as it remains a very vivid memory. This could explain my dislike of heights (particularly, as in, falling from) and tight spaces. For this reason it would be many years until my second encounter and that second meeting would be to encourage my new husband's assemblage of all things Lewis Carroll.

The journey began in 1984 after our marriage and subsequent move to the Republic of Korea. While my husband was at work I would take a taxi to downtown Seoul and peruse the antiquarian bookstores. I learned to recognize the title *Alice's Adventures in Wonderland* in *hangul* and spent hours in search of Korean *Alices*. It was an audacious adventure as the language barrier in 1984 in Seoul was a huge drawback and the fact that most bookstores in the winter months were not heated made it even more of a challenge. I would ask the bookseller, as best I could in Korean, if he had any *Alice in Wonderland* books and the answer would, invariably, be "No". I learned that persistence was a large part of success in collecting. Regardless of the negative answer, I would usually find at least one copy. Collecting is much like a treasure hunt, but without maps. You don't know where you might find one but when you do, there is great satisfaction. It was a miracle that I never had frostbitten toes or had gotten lost and ended up in North Korea, but I had discovered the joy and obsession of collecting.

During our time in Korea, we decided to write, illustrate and, try to get published a Korean adaptation of *Alice*. I enjoyed the many hours of research into Korean culture and literature and tried to stay true to the Korean implementation of verse and prose. Traditional Korean literature has its roots in folktales and we felt that the story of *Alice* would easily acculturate to a Korean version. It took a little over a year, but our endeavor was realized with the publication of *An, Sun-Hee's Adventures Under the Land of Morning Calm* (a copy of which is included in this exhibition).

Upon returning to the US, we had made the conscious decision to re-establish a Lewis Carroll collection. I encouraged Byron to publish his abandoned, monumental work, *Much of a Muchness*, a comprehensive, ten-years-in-the-making, bibliography of the American editions of the *Alice* books. I recognized the significance and importance that my husband had in his involvement with collecting Lewis Carroll and in his relationships with his acquaintances in the various Lewis Carroll Societies. This wonderfully eclectic, accomplished and diverse group of people, who have little more in common than the distinction of being Carrollians, had become an integral part of his life. Some of his great joys have been in collaborating with noted Carrollians, including August A. Imholtz, Jr., Claire Imholtz, Alan and Alison

Tannenbaum, Mark Burstein, and Edward Wakeling, among others.

Throughout the next 30 years we enjoyed collecting on a massive scale. Our Dining Room had become the Library and many, if not most, of our creative efforts have been Carroll related. Along with our Korean adaptation and several other collaborations, Byron has, arguably, written and/or illustrated more Carrollian-inspired parodies, pastiches, adaptations, fantasies, crime fiction and science fiction novellas than any other author. Some of these creative works are inspired by other works by Lewis Carroll, namely, *The Hunting of the Snark*, *Alice Through the Looking-Glass* and the *Sylvie and Bruno* books.

More recently, we collaborated on an Appalachian version of *Alice,* entitled *Alice's Adventures in an Appalachian Wonderland,* which was "translated" into the Southern Mountain dialect, as the folk speech of Appalachia is referred to by linguists. It was written in tribute to my mother, Mildred Russell Stanley Gross, who was an, approximately, 8th generation West Virginian (and Virginian, since West Virginia was formerly a western part of Virginia). Embedded in the thread of the story were memories of trips to Turkey Creek, WV where her family settled and dinners that included squirrel, homemade cornbread, apple pie, and baked beans. The book relays fond memories of fresh mountain air, warm quilts, the sweet smell in the tobacco barn, skipping rocks, and the tradition of studying the fur of "wooly bear" caterpillars to determine the course of winter. The intention was to transport the reader into the rich Appalachian culture. The choice of using the native dialect to tell the story was not embraced by some who read the original drafts, but we felt it was important to present the story in the form of a recitation. The intention was to read it as if sitting on a country porch and listening to the re-telling of a folktale (a copy of this book, along with several original illustrations, are included in this exhibition). It was in moments like this, the creative aspect of collecting, that kept our interest going for over 30 years.

We are entering a different phase of our lives, but I feel certain collecting Lewis Carroll will still play a part. It is an honor to share our love for collecting and encourage children to discover books, though perhaps, not to the excessive extent that we have done. Our children and grandchildren know the tale of *Alice* well and have shared this experience. In sharing our collection, we want to pass on the love, not only of reading, but of holding a book, turning the pages, and falling into a curious, wonderful world of adventure and fantasy.

"I almost wish I hadn't gone down that rabbit-hole—and yet—and yet—it's rather curious, you know, this sort of life!"

—Lewis Carroll

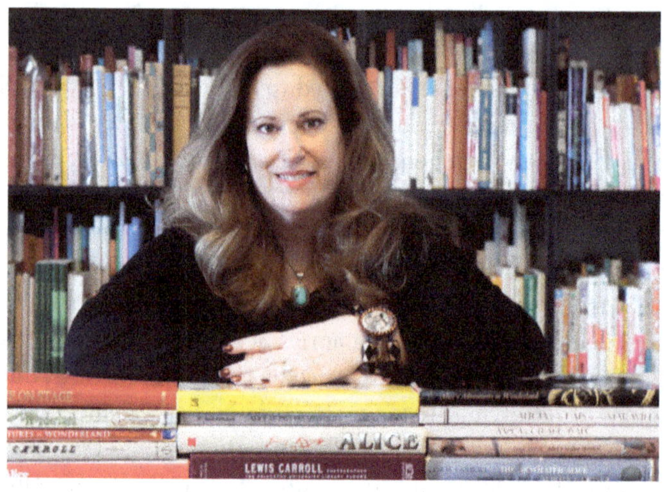

Collecting Lewis Carroll

BYRON W. SEWELL

I became interested in Lewis Carroll in 1971 after reading Martin Gardner's *The Annotated Alice*. That interest led to my building a relatively large Lewis Carroll collection, which in 1984 I donated to the Harry Ransom Humanities Research Center at the University of Texas at Austin, where I had studied fine arts. Having given away the collection I pursued other interests, the primary one being my new wife, Victoria. On the way to an extended business assignment in South Korea, we were married in an on-campus chapel at the University of New Mexico in Albuquerque, where I had earned my Chemical Engineering degree (1965). The first six months in Korea were spent in Seoul. Even though I had turned my back on Carroll, Victoria turned me back around when she spent a good part of her spare time searching for old editions of *Alice's Adventures in Wonderland* translated into Korean. She was quite good at this, and by the time we moved to a new location on the southern tip of the Korean peninsula she had located about 75 editions. This was no small feat when you realize that she spoke just a little Korean and could only recognize the title *Alice's Adventures in Wonderland* in Hangul script and most of the secondhand book dealers couldn't speak English.

Our new location was quite remote and during times when I wasn't at work we had little to do and we decided that we should create a version of *Alice* featuring a young Korean girl in traditional costume, with the scenes and characters transposed into Korea and Korean culture, and then see if we could get it translated and published. Making a long story very short, that book, *An, Sun-hee's Adventures under the Land of Morning Calm*, was eventually translated into Korean and published. Victoria wrote the English adaptation and we both worked on the illustrations.

On our return to America we decided to build another Carroll collection, the result of which includes a selection of works in this current exhibition at the Huntington Museum of Art. The Victoria Jon Sewell Lewis Carroll Collection is relatively large, though not by any means the size of some of the world's largest collections. There are over 4,800 cataloged items in her collection, though a good part of that are manuscripts and illustrations for the dozens of Carrollian things I have produced over the last 40+ years. To put this collection in perspective, the largest Carroll collection of which I am aware is held by Edward Wakeling (who wrote the preface in this catalogue), a prominent English Carrollian author as well as a major collector. The last time I asked him about its size he told me that it holds about 40,000 items and is still growing. Embedded in his collection is also the world's largest collection of my own Carrollian efforts. A few of my own pieces are included in this exhibition, some of which have been published by Michael Everson of Evertype, an Irish publisher who in part specializes in publishing Carroll, and is the publisher of this exhibition catalogue.

Recently I have heard Victoria explain to people that, even though she likes Carroll, she is not nearly as obsessed with it as I have been, and she actually encouraged me to start collecting, writing and illustrating Carrollian themed things again, because she realized that I enjoyed it so much. Such is the nature of true love. Some of the fruit of her selflessness is on display here at the HMoA today and she is absolutely the only reason this exhibition is possible.

Victoria's collection includes all manner of Carrollian items, with an expected emphasis in the standard editions, but also with significant holdings of Carroll in translation, parodies, fantasies, science-fiction, crime fiction, and the performing arts (cinema, theatre, music, dance, etc.). The selections in this exhibition reflect some of those aspects.

This exhibition is part of the national celebrations of the 150th anniversary of the first publication of *Alice's Adventures in Wonderland* in 1865, sponsored and encouraged by The Lewis Carroll Society of North America. Due to this fact the emphasis in this exhibition at the HMoA has been largely limited to the *Alice* books. However, the world of Lewis Carroll is very broad, since Carroll was so prolific. This exhibition bypasses many of these other, often equally interesting things, such as his classic epic nonsense poem, *The Hunting of the Snark*, and the myriad books and articles associated with his interesting life, including biographies, bibliographies, criticism, mathematics, pop culture, the arts, etc.

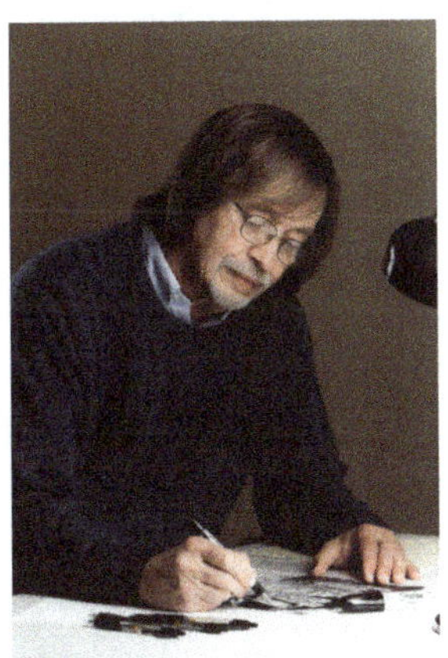

Byron Woodie Sewell

I am not alone in this keen interest in Lewis Carroll. There are a significant number of Carrollians (including many Americans), most of whom are also collectors, who are equally fascinated by Carroll. One of the joys of being a member of the LCSNA has been the friendships that I have made through the Society, and the possibility of forming these friendships, even at a distance, is one of the primary reasons I can heartily endorse joining in on the fun and becoming a member. There is so much Lewis Carroll material now available on sites such as eBay and AbeBooks that it is possible for anyone to form a nice collection even if he or she has only moderate financial means. There are at times great bargains to be had at very modest prices. The trick is to immerse oneself enough to recognize one when it appears…and then pounce!

Catalogue
of the Exhibition

With minor exceptions, this catalogue refers to Charles Lutwidge Dodgson as "Lewis Carroll" (or simply "Carroll"), the pseudonym by which he is most commonly known today. Further, *Alice* or *AAIW* is often used to refer to *Alice's Adventures in Wonderland* (or *AIW* to *Alice in Wonderland*) and *Looking-Glass* or *TTLG* is often used to refer to *Through the Looking-Glass, and What Alice Found There* (or simply *Through the Looking-Glass*).

1   Charles Lutwidge Dodgson / "Lewis Carroll". *Reflections in a Looking Glass / A Centennial Celebration of Lewis Carroll, Photographer.* This image is an assisted self-portrait (Carroll set up the camera, including a properly prepared glass plate for the negative, posed himself, and then another person briefly removed the lens cap for the timed exposure) taken in October 1876 when he was 44 years old. It was one of the last portraits taken of him and was used by the artist Hubert von Herkomer (1849–1914; German-British) when he painted Dodgson's posthumous portrait in 1899, which now hangs in the Great Hall at Christ Church. See No. 9 below. (Aperture Foundation and the Harry Ransom Humanities Research Center, 1998.)

2   "Tom Gate Ch. Ch. Oxford." This antique albumen paper print, produced from a glass negative originally taken in 1864 by an unknown photographer, was originally mounted in a Victorian album. The handwritten title refers to Christ Church (the college name, often abbreviated as "Ch. Ch.", including by Carroll) in Oxford, where Carroll lived most of his adult life (from 1868 until his death in 1898) and where he lectured on mathematics. "Tom" is the affectionate name for the large bell that hangs in the tower above the gate at the tower's base.

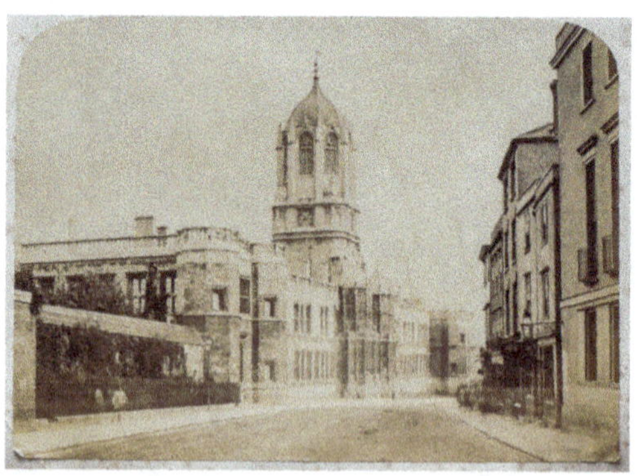

It was rung every hour on the hour, night and day. Dodgson's suite of rooms was located on both floors of the building, seen here at the very left-hand corner, situated between the two turrets. The figures in this photograph appear ghost-like due to their movement during the relatively long time required to expose a specially coated glass plate to sunlight.

3   *Symbolic Logic / Part 1 / Elementary.* Dodgson wrote numerous books on various mathematical topics. He was especially interested in the field of logic and even taught it to some of his numerous child-friends. The copy exhibited here was published shortly before his death on the 18th of January 1898. (London: Macmillan, 1897, fourth edition.)

4   "Alice Pleasance Liddell as a beggar girl." The photograph depicted here (in an auction catalogue) was taken by Dodgson (ca. 1858 or 1859). It is believed to have been hand-colored by him. Morton Cohen (1922–; American), Lewis Carroll's most authoritative modern biographer, regards this image as the most memorable and iconic photograph that Carroll ever took. The beggar costume belies the fact that Alice, like Dodgson, was a member of the upper classes, though Alice was at a somewhat higher level. (*Lewis Carroll's Alice / The Photographs, Books, Papers and Personal Effects of Alice Liddell and Her Family.* Sotheby's / London [catalogue] June 6, 2001, Sale LO1912; inscribed by a representative of the heirs of the family estate).

5   The 1858 Dodgson photograph depicted in this book is of the three Liddell sisters: Edith Mary (b. 1853), Lorina Charlotte (b. 1849), and Alice Pleasance (b. 1852). In the Prefatory poem in *Alice,* Lorina is "Prima", Alice is "Secunda", and Edith is "Tertia". (*Lewis Carroll.* London and NY: Phaidon, 2008.)

6   The 1860 Dodgson photograph depicted in this book is of Alice Liddell. Dodgson clipped an oval of Alice's head from a print of this same photograph and glued it to the last page of the original hand-written and illustrated manuscript, which he entitled *Alice's Adventures Under Ground.* He eventually presented the manuscript to Alice as a memento of their boating

trip and the first telling of the famous story. Dodgson had originally drawn Alice's portrait in the manuscript, which is a good likeness, but decided to replace it with the photograph. *Lewis Carroll / Photographer / The Princeton University Library Album.* (Princeton University Press, 2002.)

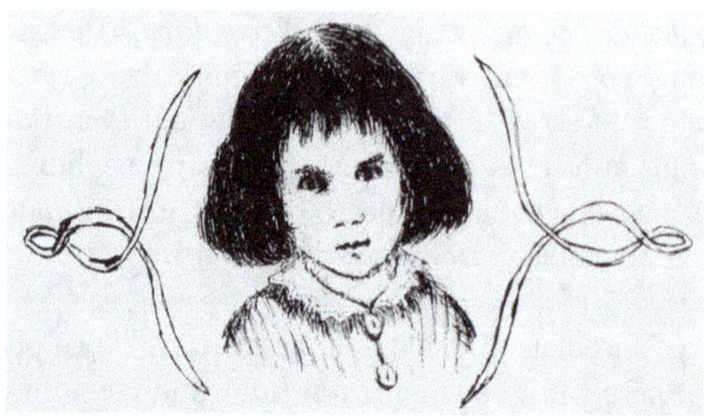

7   "View from the Boat House. Oxford." This antique albumen paper print, produced from a glass negative, was probably taken in 1864 by William Taunt (1842–1922; English), a professional Oxford photographer. The scene is the boathouse at Salter's Yard – exactly where Dodgson, his friend The Reverend Robinson Duckworth (appointed Canon of Westminster in 1875 and often referred to later as Canon Duckworth; 1834–1911; English), and the three Liddell sisters set off from on July 2, 1862. The photograph is taken from Folly Bridge looking downriver. Just to the left, behind the trees, is Christ Church Meadow and a pathway leading to Christ Church.

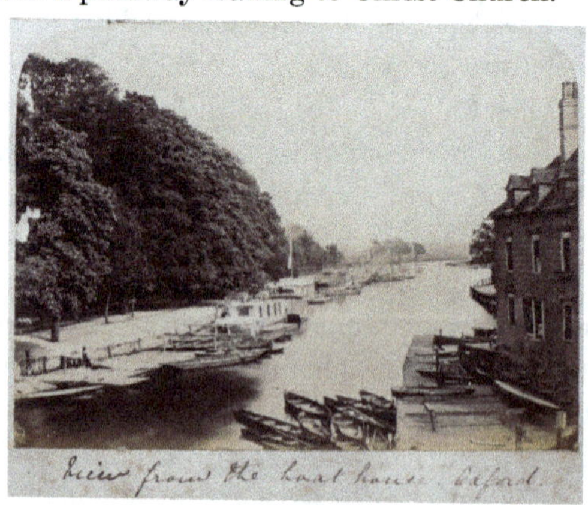

8   "Christ Church". This antique albumen paper print, reproduced from a glass negative originally taken ca. 1880–90 by an unknown photographer, was originally mounted in a Victorian album. It is a view across Christ Church Meadow. The deanery where Alice and her family lived is just behind the surrounding wall. Tom Tower can be seen in the middle distance. Christ Church Cathedral's imposing steeple is to the right. Alice's father, Henry Gordon Liddell (1811–1898; English) was Vice-Chancellor of Oxford University and Dean of Christ Church. He is rightfully renowned as one of the editors of what is typically referred to as the *Liddell & Scott Greek-English Lexicon* (first published by Clarendon Press at Oxford, 1843), but most people now associate him as being the father of Alice Liddell. Curiously, Dean Liddell does not mention Carroll in his autobiography (possibly because of the acrimonious split between Alice's parents and Dodgson). Perhaps even stranger is the fact that Dodgson and Dean Liddell died the same week: Dodgson on the 14th of January 1898 and Liddell on the 18th of January. The number (26805) in the lower left-hand corner is the handwritten serial ID number that would have appeared on the photographer's original glass negative plate.

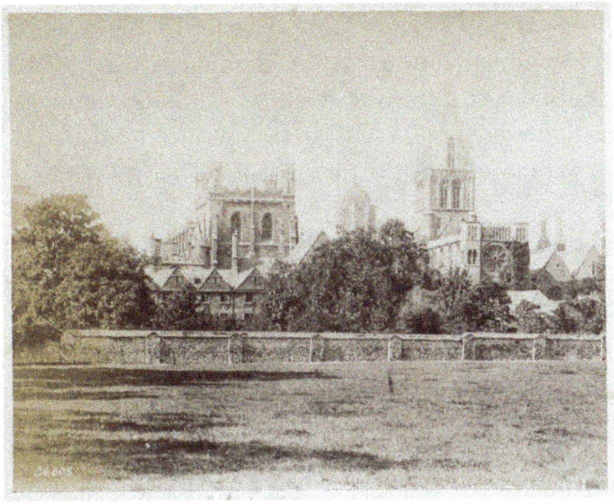

9   "Christ Church Dining Hall / Oxford." This antique albumen paper print, reproduced from a glass negative originally taken ca. 1880–90 by an unknown photographer, was originally mounted in a Victorian album. It is a view of the Great Hall where Dodgson would have taken most of his meals. Today the hall is also famous as having been used as the model for the great hall in the Harry Potter films.

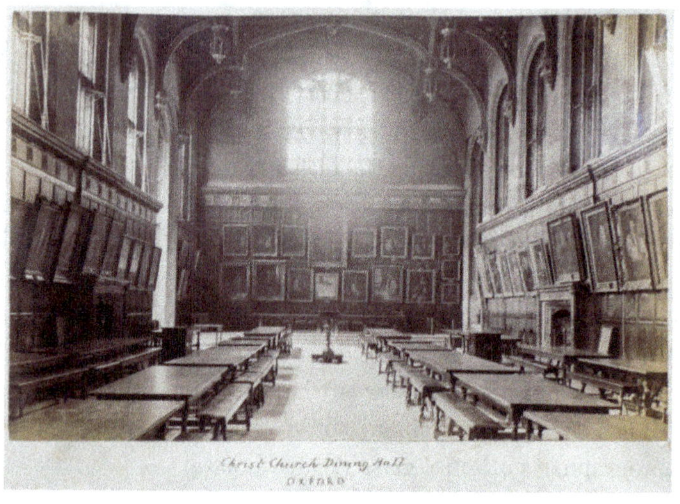

10   "Tom Quad, Christ Church, Oxford." This ca. 1900–20 "real photograph postcard" (a continuous-tone photographic image printed on postcard stock) is of the Quadrangle around which the buildings for Christ Church are located. Dodgson's rooms were located at the far right-hand corner of this view.

11   *Alice's Adventures Under Ground.* This facsimile of Carroll's original manuscript book was issued as part of the celebration of the centenary of his birth in 1932. (NY: Macmillan, 1932; reprint of the 1886 first edition.) He presented the manuscript to Alice on November 26, 1864, having dedicated it as "A Christmas Gift to a Dear Child in Memory of a Summer's Day." Carroll borrowed the original manuscript from Alice (by then, Mrs. Reginald Hargreaves) in order to have it photographed for

the production of the first facsimile edition in 1886. He had great difficulty with the photographer, who eventually had to be taken to court before producing all of the plates. Some Carrollian experts, including Martin Gardner (1914–2010; American), author of *The Annotated Alice* (1965), speculate that an earlier version of the manuscript was destroyed by Dodgson after he wrote a more elaborate version, including the addition of the episodes about the Cheshire Cat and the Mad Tea-Party. The original version of the story had been expanded from 15,500 to 27,500 words by the time *Alice* was first published in 1865.

12   There have been a number of later facsimile editions of *Alice's Adventures Under Ground*. Of special note is this "micro-miniature" bound edition privately printed by Lewis Carroll collectors Alan (1951–; American) and Alison Tannenbaum (1946–; American) in 2012 in an edition limited to fifty copies for private distribution. It is enclosed in a small hinged clear snap-box, which is itself contained in a small fabric bag. The full text is legible, though most of us would require a magnifying glass to read it. The book's size can be understood in comparison with the West Virginia state quarter placed nearby.

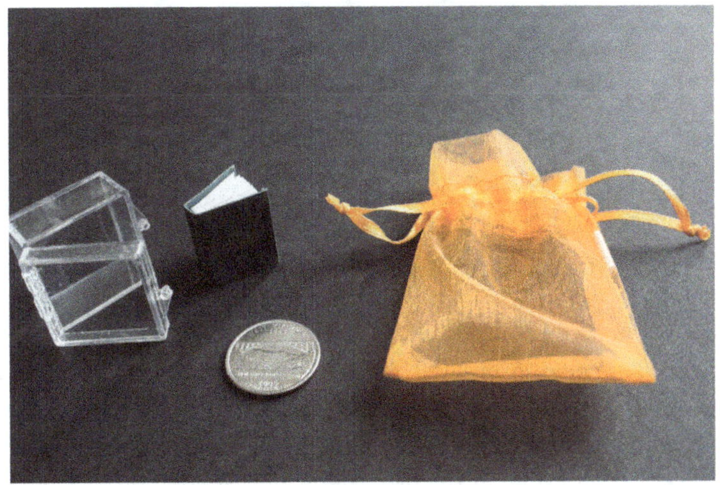

13   *Square Alice*. Carroll suffered from insomnia and in order to allow himself to "write" in complete darkness under the bedcovers he invented a device that he called the "Nyctograph", basically a small template with rows of square holes which facilitated marking either dots or short lines with a pencil. This is what Carroll said about his invention in the October 1891 issue of *The Lady*: "*Anyone who has tried, as I have often done, the process of getting out of bed at 2 a.m. in a winter night, lighting a candle, and recording some happy thought which would probably be otherwise forgotten, will agree with me it entails much discomfort. All I have now to do, if I wake and think of something I wish to record, is to draw from under the pillow a small memorandum book containing my Nyctograph, write a few lines, or even a few pages, without even putting the hands outside the bed-clothes, replace the book, and go to sleep again.*"

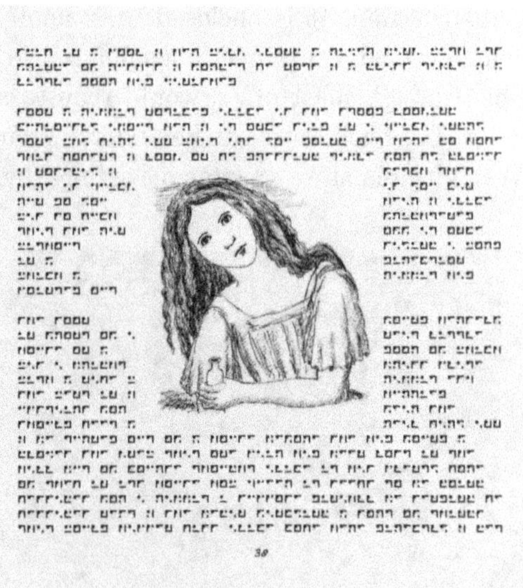

Alan Tannebaum created a nyctographic font and used it to transliterate this curious edition of *Alice's Adventures Under Ground* into Carroll's "Nyctographic Square Alphabet". Jacob Levernier, writing on the blog *Sparks for Inquiry* on the 12th of January 2012, explains the etymology of "nyctograph" as having come from Hellenistic Greek, meaning "writing by night", and points out that there was a French machine enabling the blind to write or the sighted to write in the dark called the *nyctographe* (1818– 19, or earlier). (Privately published by Alan Tannebaum, 2005.)

14   地下の国のアリス (*Chika no kuni no Arisu; Arisu in Under Ground*). This Japanese edition of *Alice's Adventures Under Ground* was translated by Izumi Yasui. (Tokyo: Shinshokan, 2005.) Lewis Carroll is immensely popular in Japan and there have been literally hundreds of Japanese editions of *Alice* and *Looking-Glass*. However, only three different translations of *Alice's Adventures Under Ground* have appeared, of which the first was in 1987.

15   *Alice's Adventures in Wonderland.* (London: Macmillan, 1869, 14th thousand). Illustrated by John Tenniel (1820–1914; English). Early editions of *Alice* are prized by Carroll collectors and copies in reasonably good condition are typically expensive. There are only 21 known extant copies of the 1865 first edition (at this writing) and they can command prices of up to $1,000,000 when they very occasionally appear on the market.

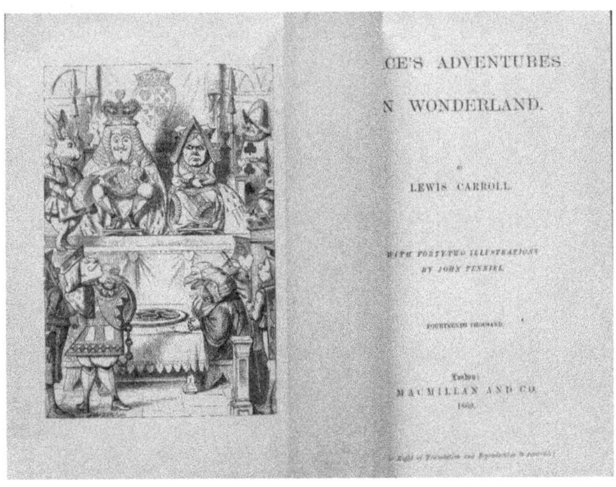

The reason for the great rarity of the 1865 edition is that even though there were 2,000 copies printed, fewer than fifty were bound before Tenniel expressed his dissatisfaction with the printing, causing Carroll to scrap the edition and reprint. He asked those to whom he had presented copies to return them for replacement. Some did and most of those returned he gave away to children's hospitals and reading rooms where most were eventually destroyed by heavy use. As a result, one of the great book rarities of all time was created. People of normal financial means can hardly aspire to owning copies of even the 1866 edition. The 1869 edition exhibited here is more in the realm of affordability for most people. This copy was once in the collection of Denis Crutch (now deceased), who was the final editor of *The Lewis Carroll Handbook* (1979), which remains the most authoritative guide to Lewis Carroll materials, though now in need of yet another update.

16   *Alice's Adventures in Wonderland.* This presentation copy is inscribed by Carroll on the half-title as: *"Alice Emily Shute _ presented by the Author—in memory of an evening in Theatrical Wonderland, and of the 'Dirge of Dundee'—Dec. 29. 1869."*

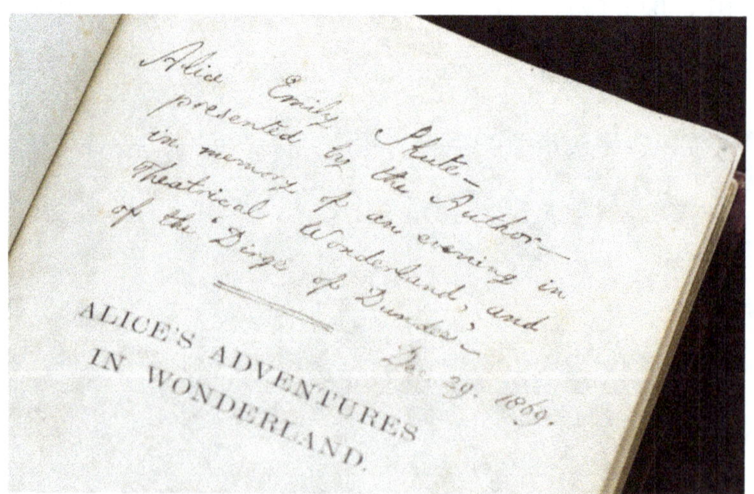

This incident is specifically mentioned in Dodgson's *Diaries* for December 27 as follows: *Theatrical performance at Mr. Synge's very enjoyable. The treat of the evening to me, was the "Dirge over Dundee," sung by Alice Shute, to the tune of "Ye banks and braes," unaccompanied, and with a perfectly true and deliciously sweet voice.* (London: Macmillan, 1869, 18th thousand.)

17   *Alice's Adventures in Wonderland.* (Boston: Lee and Shepard / NY: Lee Shepard and Dillingham, 1871.) Rather than shred them, the rejected sheets of the first (1865) printing were shipped to New York, where they were sold to D. Appleton and Co., who bound them with a new title page. These copies were for sale only in the United States. Copies of this edition are known as "Appleton *Alices*". Though they utilize the first edition sheets, they are far more common than the true bound first editions and command much more moderate prices today.

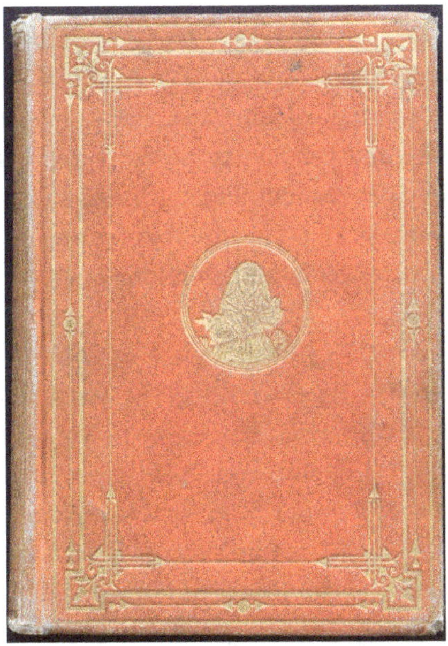

The first edition of *Alice* actually printed in America was by Lee & Shepard in 1869. Because of the state of copyright laws, no permission was needed to print these American editions. The Lee & Shepard copy exhibited here has an unusually elaborate gilt-stamped cover design.

18 *Through the Looking Glass, and What Alice Found There.* Carroll spent several years preparing this sequel to *Alice*, which was published in time for the 1871 Christmas market. The first American edition exhibited here was produced by Macmillan in London and shipped to Lee & Shepard. In a strange bibliographical twist, the initial shipment consisting of 2,000 copies (printed at the same time as the first English edition) may have actually been available in America a few days before the Macmillan version was published in London, and if true, can arguably claim to have been the first edition available to the public. (Boston: Lee and Shepard / NY: Lee Shepard and Dillingham, 1872.)

19 *Through the Looking Glass, and What Alice Found There.* This is the first English edition. By 1871 *Alice* had established such popularity that *Looking-Glass* was published in an edition of 9,000 copies, and yet had to be reprinted before the end of 1872. This copy has a small folded leaflet, a Christmas greeting "To All Child-readers of *Alice in Wonderland*" tipped in on the front paste-down. (London: Macmillan, 1872.)

20–21 (20): *A Wreath of Song / for Children / Containing / the Songs from "Alice in Wonderland" / The Songs from "Through the Looking-Glass". Words by Kingsley, Procter, MacDonald, Dr. Nield, Herrik,..."* (London: Weeks & Co., ca. 1896.) *"The Songs from Alice"* and *The Songs from Looking-Glass"* were first published separately by Weeks in 1870 & 1872, respectively. Song-books (like the one in this exhibition) contain settings for Carroll's poetry by William Boyd. Many of Carroll's poems were actually parodies of existing songs, but these songs introduced new music for twelve of his poems.

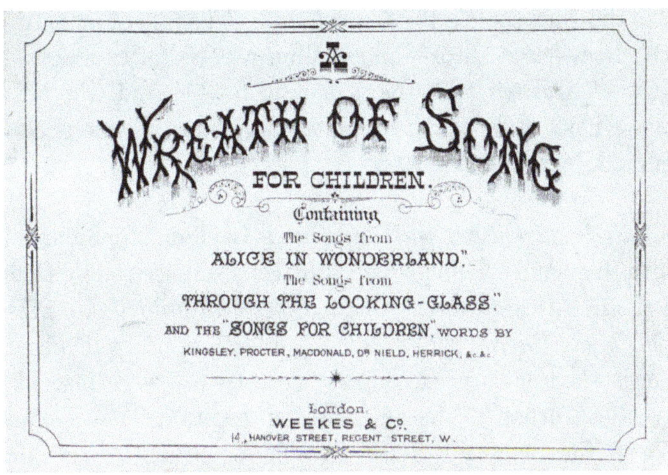

(21): There have been a very large number of versions of Carroll's works put to music over the decades. This relatively modern example is based upon Chapter IV, "Tweedledum and Tweedledee" from *Looking-Glass*. The sheet music features words by Carroll and music by Percy E. Fletcher.

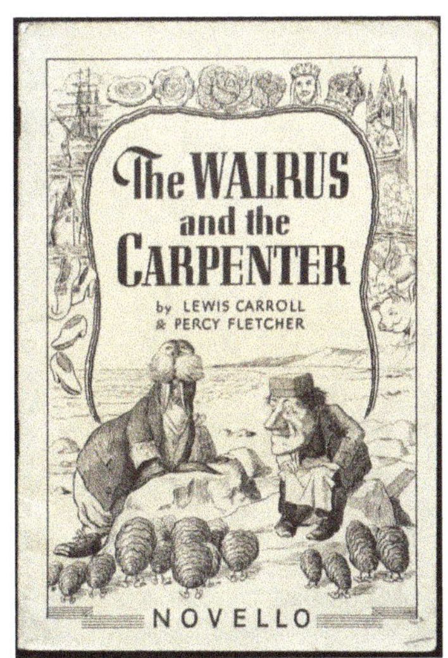

The wraps are decorated with one of Sir John Tenniel's iconic illustrations. The border features objects from the famous poem:

"The time has come", the Walrus said, / "To talk of many things: / Of shoes—and ships—and sealing wax—/ Of cabbages—and kings—/ And why the sea is boiling hot—/ And whether pigs have wings." (*The Walrus and the Carpenter*, London: Novello, undated, but probably 1971).

22 *Alice's Adventures in Wonderland*. London: Macmillan, 1879 (60th thousand). This presentation copy is inscribed by Dodgson on the half-title page to: "*Jessie Coles / an unbirthday present / from Lewis Carroll / Sep. 22/79*". Inscriptions by Dodgson as "Lewis Carroll" are exceedingly rare (many were inscribed as "by the Author"). Jessie Coles is mentioned in Dodgson's *Diaries* for Sept. 20, 1879 as follows: "Fetched over Jessie, Beatrice and Amy Coles for an hour, and showed them chromograph, etc." A "chromograph" is an apparatus by which a number of copies of written matter, maps, etc. can be made. Most of his life Dodgson notoriously strove to hide the fact that he and Carroll were the same person from anyone except his close circle of family and friends. The "unbirthday gift" in the presentation is a reference to Humpty Dumpty's conversation with Alice in *Looking-Glass*.

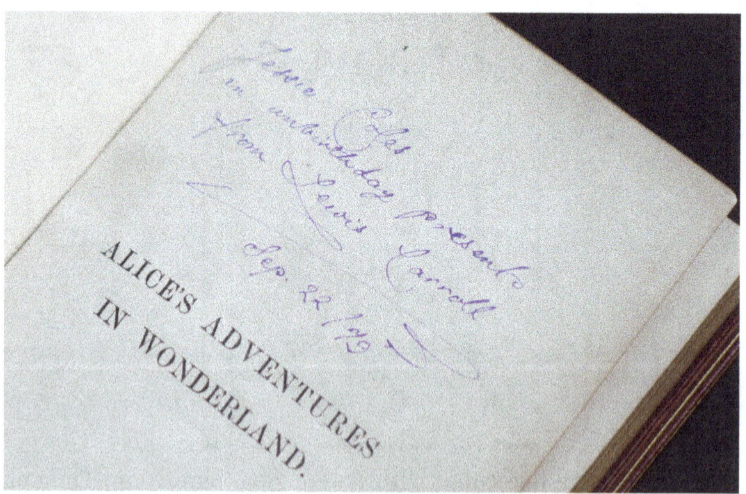

This copy was rebound decades ago in gilt-stamped brown leather with Tenniel figures by renowned London bookbinders Sangorski and Sutcliffe. Tipped into the book is an 1856 autograph letter (one sheet, written on both sides) in John Tenniel's hand. This copy of *Alice* was inherited by a relative of the last wife of George T. Delacorte, Jr. on her death. Delacorte founded the Dell Publishing Co. and was the philanthropist who donated the funds for the iconic "Alice in Wonderland" statue in NYC's Central Park as a memorial to his first wife whom he said was especially fond of *Alice*. Dell was the early publisher of Walt Disney comic books, including the early *Alice in Wonderland* comics associated with the 1951 Disney movie.

23   *Alice's Adventures in Wonderland and Through the Looking-Glass* [together in one volume] / *People's Edition*. Once the popularity of the *Alice* books was established, Carroll decided to issue editions that would be more affordable for the lower classes. He made numerous corrections to the text for these editions, and though his original intent was to eliminate the illustrations, Macmillan convinced him that the books should contain all the original pictures. The People's Editions, first published in green pictorial bindings in 1887, were immensely popular and have remained in print to this day. (London: Macmilan, 1892.) In the past few years even these originally inexpensive editions have begun to command surprisingly high prices.

24   *The Nursery Alice*. As early as 1881, Carroll had wanted to produce an edition of *Alice* for very young children. For this version he adapted the text and Tenniel redrew twenty of the illustrations in color, giving Alice a bright yellow and dark blue dress (the blue dress many people around the world associate with Alice is probably due to the overwhelming influence of the Walt Disney animated film). One wonders if Tenniel might have been inspired by Peter Paul Rubens' famous self-portrait with his family, *Rubens with His Wife Hélène Fourment and Their Son Frans* (ca. 1635; now hanging in the Metropolitan Museum of

Art, NY), which depicts his young son wearing a very similar bright yellow and blue style costume that resembles a dress. Carroll felt that the illustrations in the first printing of *The Nursery Alice* were too bright for the sensitive eyes of small English children and so the edition was rejected! These unacceptably gaudy copies were shipped off to America, because of the belief that the eyes of American children were not quite as sensitive. Thus, in a curious bibliographical twist, though the book was first printed in 1889, the American edition represents the first publication of the original English sheets. A new edition with "superior" (subdued) coloring was quickly published in London in March 1890 for the English market. *The Nursery Alice* did not sell well, perhaps due to the condescending tone of the text (or too bright color?), and has only been reprinted occasionally. Fine copies of this book exist, but many, if not most, are in similarly well-worn condition as the copy exhibited here, ample evidence that they had spent a good part of their existence in nurseries before passing into collections where they are now much better taken care of. (NY: Macmillan, 1890; first American edition.)

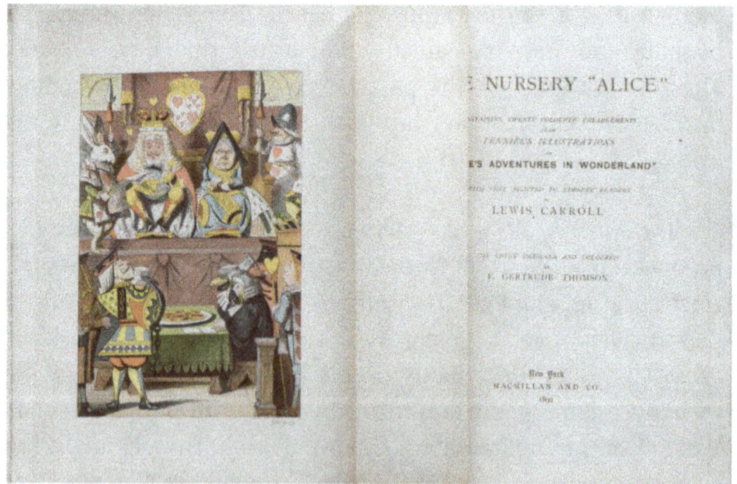

25   This modern poster reproduces Tenniel's illustration for Chapter IX, "The Cheshire Cat", from *The Nursery Alice*.

26   *Приключения Алисы в Стране чудес, рассказанные для маленьких читателей самим автором* [*Priključenija Alisy v Strane čudes, rasskazannye dlja malen'kix čitatelej samim avtorom; The Nursery Alice*]. Translated into Russian by Nina M. Demurova, a famed contemporary translator and literary critic. It is spectacularly illustrated by Elena Bazanova. (St. Petersburg: "Речь", 2012.)

27   *Приключения Алисы в Стране чудес / Алиса в Зазеркалье. (Priključenija Alisy v Strane čudes / Alisa v Zazerkal'e [AAIW / TTLG]*). This early copy of Nina Demurova's famous translation of *Alice's Adventures in Wonderland* and *Through the Looking-glass* is humorously inscribed by her on the title page as: "For Byron Sewell—Please, don't be put off by the cover. The inside is a lot better, I think—N. Demmurova April, 2005". The illustrations are by Irina Kazakova. (Petrozavodsk: Karelia Publications, 1979).

28   子供部屋のアリス (*Kodomobeya no Arisu; Arisu in Nursery* [*The Nursery Alice*]). Translated into Japanese by Yasunari Takahashi and Michi Takahashi. This edition is illustrated with the original Tenniel illustrations. (Tokyo: Shinshokan, 2003.)

29   *The Wonderland Postage Stamp Case.* Decorated front and back with Tenniel's image of Alice holding the pig-baby (on the front) and the Cheshire Cat (on the back). The case and postage stamp insert are a simple, but clever, device. When the insert is pulled out (especially if done quickly) the baby that Alice is holding seems to turn into a pig, and from the other side when the insert is pulled out the Cheshire Cat seems to largely disappear. Inserted in the stamp case and sprinkled around it are franked (canceled) Victorian stamps of various denominations, consistent with the period. Of course, in Victorian times the stamps would have been new, not franked, as

here. The first edition was published by Emberlin and Son, Oxford in 1890. The example in this exhibition is a ca. 1907 reprint that has darkened with age.

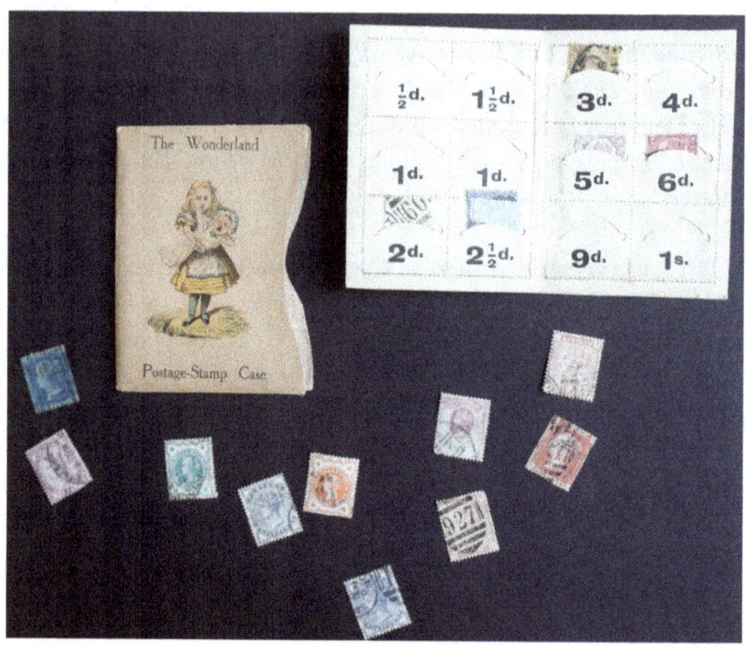

30   This is an example of a contemporary letter envelope (referred to as a "cover" by philatelists). It was posted on May 3, 1862, just a few weeks earlier than the day Carroll told the Liddell sisters about Alice's adventures underground (July 4, 1862). Carroll would have recognized these Victorian stamps. The proper philatelic description of this cover is: "Great Britain / Queen Victoria Issue". Scott #20. Posted May 3, 1862 from London, to Rouen, France." It is mounted in a polyethylene protective sleeve on a modern Great Britain postage stamp album sheet.

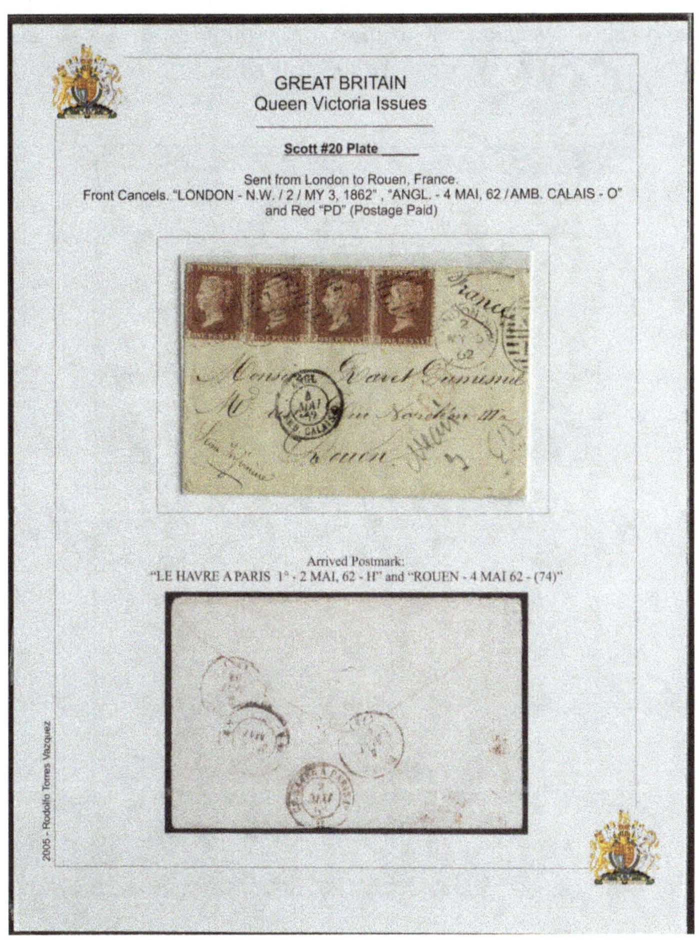

31   *Alice's Adventures in Wonderland.* Illustrated by Blanche McManus (1870–1935; American). Although a few scattered illustrations of *Alice* by artists other than Tenniel had appeared before 1899, this edition of *Alice* represents the first fully and originally illustrated edition by another artist before the expiration of the 1907 English copyright. Since it was unauthorized, it was not for sale in Great Britain. The plate showing Alice falling down the rabbit hole depicts, hanging on the wall of the deep shaft at the upper left-hand, what is perhaps

the earliest version of a map of Wonderland. (NY: M. F. Mansfield and A. Wessels, 1890; first edition.)

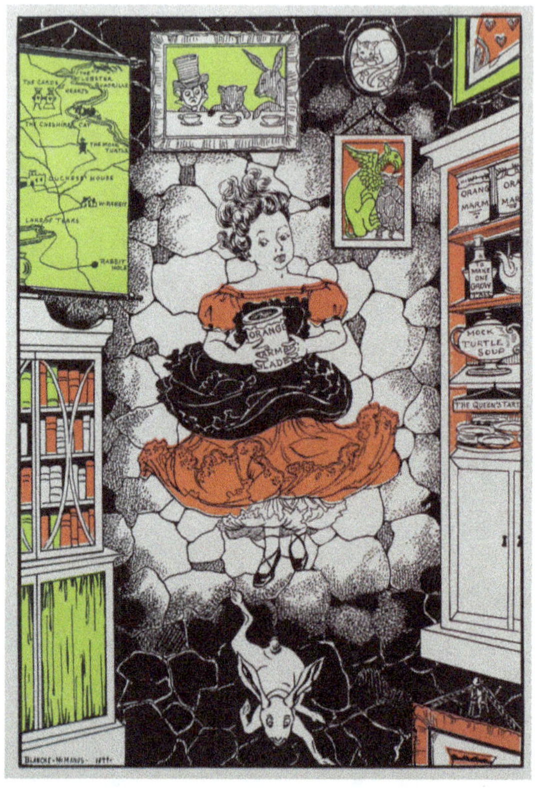

32   *Alice's Adventures in Wonderland*. Illustrated by Milicent Sowerby (1878–1967; American.) Sowerby's illustrations were used for the first illustrated *Alice* by an artist other than Tenniel after the expiration of the 1907 copyright. The copy in this exhibition is the first American edition with Sowerby's illustrations. (NY: Duffield and London: Chatto and Windus, 1908.)

33–34 (33): *Alice's Adventures in Wonderland*. Illustrated by Arthur Rackham (1867–1939; English). Rackham's illustrations were the first to provide a completely new view of Wonderland, revealing something of the nightmarish side of

Alice. He received some harsh criticism from reviewers for challenging Tenniel and for that reason declined to illustrate *Looking-Glass*, though Macmillan offered the opportunity to do so even though the book was still under copyright. Today, Rackham's illustrations are among the most admired and readily recognized after Tenniel's and have been frequently reprinted. The edition in this exhibition is the First American trade edition (NY: Duffield and London: Chatto and Windus, 1908). (34): This modern poster beautifully reproduces Arthur Rackham's illustration for Chapter III, "A Caucus-Race and a Long Tale", from *Alice*.

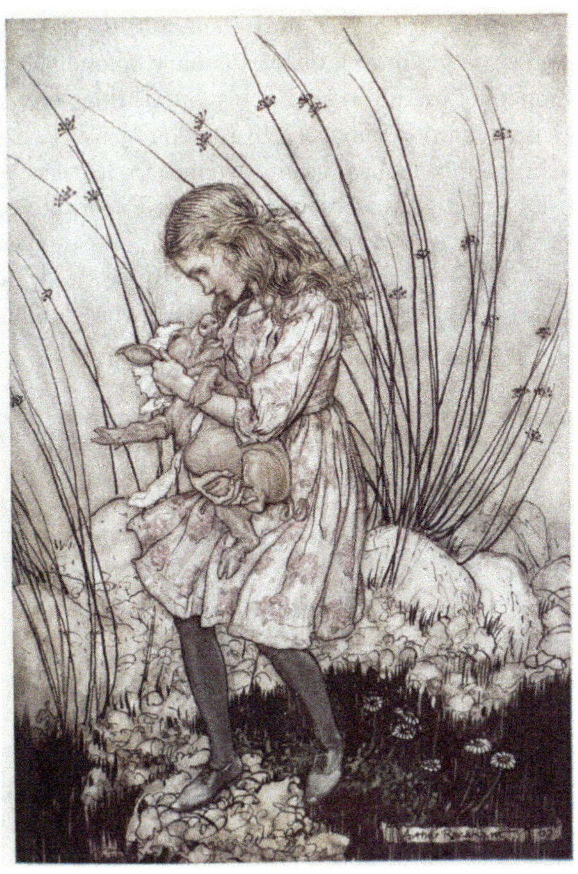

35   *Alice im Wunderland* [*AIW*]. Illustrated by Arthur Rackham. Translated into German by Helene Scheu-Riesz. This is the first German edition with Rackham's illustrations for *Alice*. (Weimar: Verlag von Gustav Kiepenheuer, 1912.) This copy, inscribed by Alise Wagner to Byron Sewell, was at one time in her collection. Alise [pseudonym] G. Wagner (Gisela Wagner née Seubert; 1944–; German) is co-editor of *The German Alice / An Annotated Bibliography*. (Dortmund: privately published, 2005.)

36   *La aventuroj de Alicio en Mirlando* [*AAIW*]. Illustrated by Brinsley Le Fanu (Irish; 1854–1929). Translated into Esperanto by E. L. Kearney. The copy exhibited here is the first edition of *Alice* translated into Esperanto, the most widely spoken constructed international auxiliary language (created by L. L. Zamenhof in 1887). Le Fanu's illustrations first appeared in 1907 in an edition published in London by W. T. Stead. The copy exhibited here has been rebound in leather. (London: British Esperanto Association, 1910; first Esperanto edition.)

37   *Alice's Adventures in Wonderland*. Illustrated by Bessie Pease (Gutman) (1876–1960; American). Pease's illustrations were first published in 1907 in NY by Dodge.

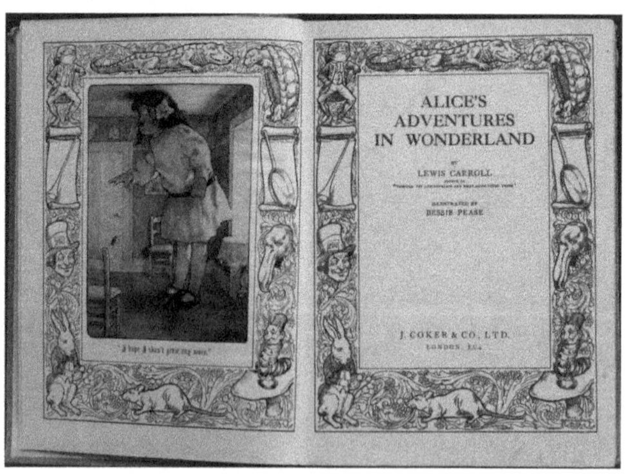

Pease's illustrations for *Alice* are most memorable for the youth of Alice, who is most often portrayed older than her seven-and-a-half years. Pease gives the viewer an Alice who can't be much older than four. This copy is a late reprint. (London: J. Coker, ca. 1930.)

38   *Alice's Adventures in Wonderland.* Illustrated by W[illiam] H. Walker (British; ?). (London: John Lane the Bodley Head, 1907.)

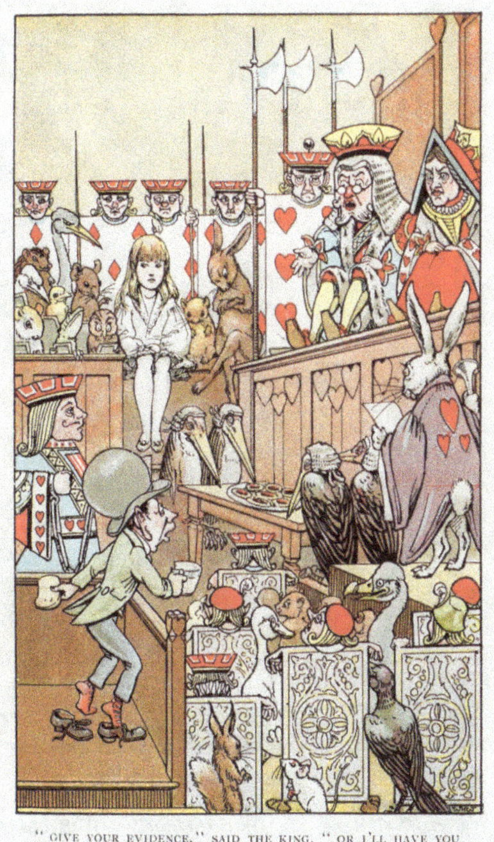

39–40 (39): *Alice im Wunderland* [*Alice in Wonderland*]. Illustrated by A. E. Jackson (color plates) and Kurt Lange (black and white line illustrations). Jackson (1873–1952; English) depicts more of the landscape of Wonderland than most illustrators, with lush details filled in behind the scenes. The cover design is wonderful (superior to the later American edition), but the quality of the color plates is much inferior. (Berlin: Meidinger's Jungenschriften Verlag, [1931]; first German edition with Jackson illustrations.)

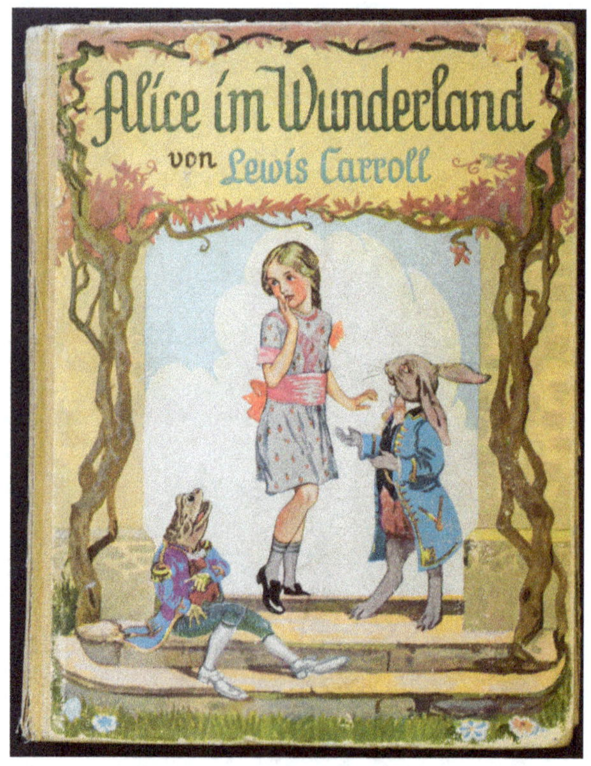

(40): *Alice's Adventures in Wonderland*. Illustrated by A. E. Jackson. (Garden City, NY: Garden City Pubishing, undated: ca. 1914).

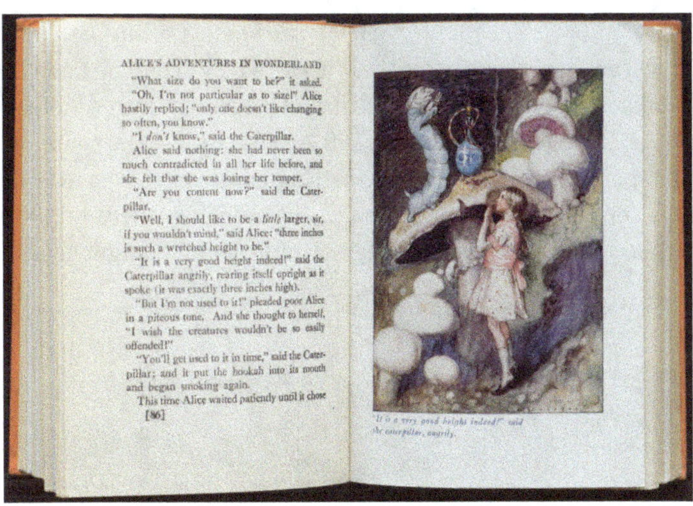

41   *The Wonderland Picture Book.* The cover of this book, by an unidentified illustrator, features the scene in *Alice* where the Dodo is about to present prizes after the completion of the caucus race. In spite of the title and the cover illustration, the book has no other connection to Carroll. (London: Ward Locke, ca. 1922.)

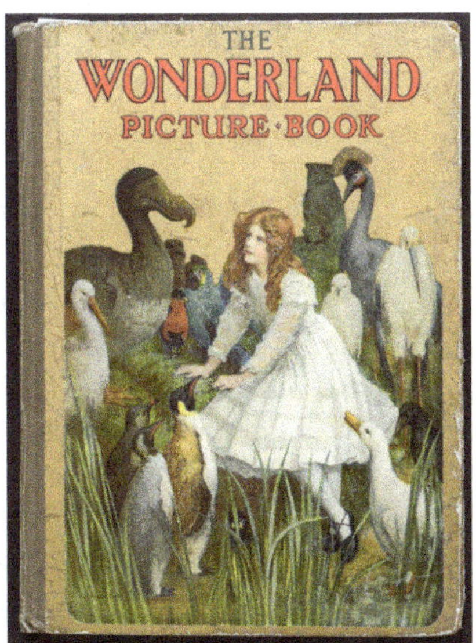

42   阿麗思漫遊奇境記 [*Ālìsī Mànyóu Qíjìng Jì; Alice's Adventures in Wonderland*]. Illustrated by Tenniel and T. H. Robinson (1869–1954; English). Translated into Chinese by Yen R. Chao (Zhào Yuánrèn, 1892–1982; Chinese), reputedly the most perfectly bilingual Chinese-English speaker who ever lived. This copy was inscribed by Chao in California where in 1952 he had become the Agassiz Professor of Oriental Languages.

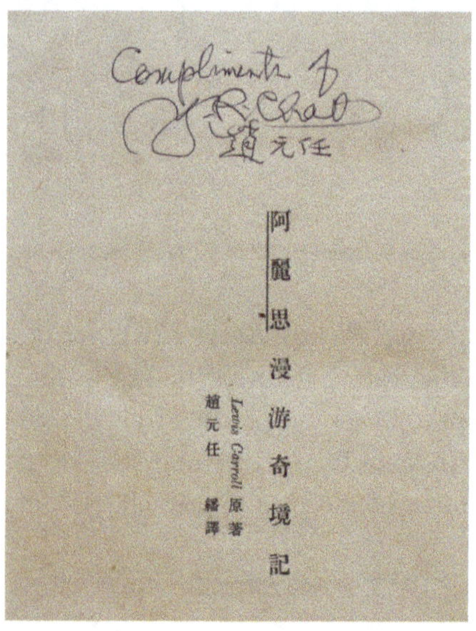

Sadly, the printing press which printed the early editions of *Alice* in Chinese was bombed by the Japanese in the Second World War, destroying all of the production plates. Robinson's illustrations were first published in 1922. Dia Liuling, writing on Chinese children's literature, notes that Chao believed that "English books could be best translated into spoken Chinese" rather than in antiquated literary Chinese. "In the case of books like *Alice in Wonderland* which was written chiefly for children, this is particularly true…For this reason he preferred living, everyday speech based on the Beijing dialect. The whole book, rich in innocent fun, parodies and nonsense rhymes, was satisfactorily rendered into Chinese." (*An Encyclopedia of Translation: Chinese-English, English-Chinese, The Chinese University Press, 2001*). Copies of the early Chinese *Alice*

editions are quite rare. Fewer than twenty copies of this 1931 printing are known to survive. (Shanghai: Commercial Press Ltd, April 1931; this edition is commonly referred to as the "5th Chinese edition".)

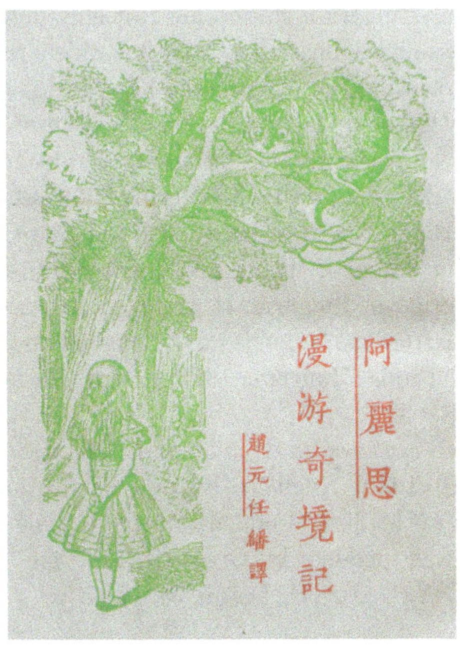

43   **אליס בארץ הפלאות** [*Alis be'eretz hapla'ot*; *Alis in the land of wonders*; *AAIW*]. Illustrated by Arthur Rackham (printed in sepia tones), and black and white line illustrations by Charles Robinson (1870–1937; English). Translated into modern Hebrew by L. Simon [born Arye Leib Semyatzki]. This is the first Hebrew edition of *Alice* and is the only Hebrew edition printed in pre-WW-I and WW-II Germany. Most copies of this edition would have been destroyed by the Nazis. Alise G. Wagner, co-editor of *The German Alice,* the standard bibliography of the German editions of Carroll, believes that there is no surviving copy of this edition in Germany. (Frankfurt, Moscow and Odessa: Omanut, 5684 A.M. by the Hebrew calendar [1923].)

44   *Алиса в страната на чудесата* [*Alisa v stranata na čydesata AAIW*]. Translated into Bulgarian by Lazar Goldman. Illustrated with black and white line illustrations by Mabel Lucy Attwell (1879–1964; English). Attwell's illustrations for *Alice* were first published in 1910 (London: Raphael Tuck.) The color plates in this Bulgarian edition are probably done in Attwell's style by a less-gifted illustrator. Attwell is widely remembered for her style of drawing featuring cherub-like figures. This manifests in *Alice* as what could be best described as "cute". According to Maria Pipeva, in her article, "Bulgarian Translations of Lewis Carroll's Works", published in the Spring 2000 issue of *The Lewis Carroll Journal*, "The translation of *Wonderland* was the most notable achievement in translated children's literature of the inter-war period in Bulgaria. It was one of the still few translations made from the language of the original and rendering the text in full." (Sofia: Чипеввъ, 1933; first Bulgarian edition.)

45   *Alice's Adventures in Wonderland.* Illustrated by George Soper (1870–1942; English). Soper's illustrations were first published by Headley (London) in 1911. The copy in this exhibition was printed in Great Britain for its American publisher. (NY: George H. Doran, ca. 1927.)

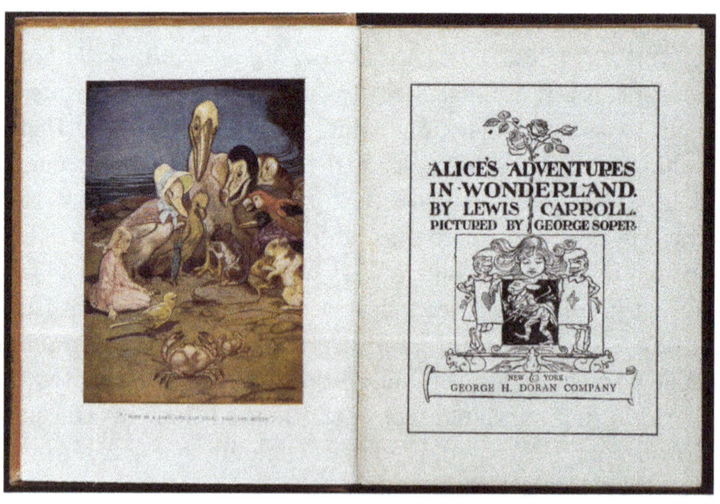

46   *Alice's Adventures in Wonderland.* Illustrated by William ("Willy") Andrew Pogany (1882–1955; Hungarian). Pogany lived most of his life in America. This spectacular edition of *Alice* is done in a classic Art Deco style. John N. S. Davis (1931–1981; English), a major Carroll collector and one of the founders of the English Lewis Carroll Society as well as one of the co-editors of the influential anthology, *The Illustrators of Alice* (London: Academy Editions, 1972), regarded Pogany's version as the first really original interpretation of *Alice* since Tenniel (though some might argue that Rackham's was the first). Alice is dressed as a flapper, the heart and diamond cards are straight out of a Ziegfeld Follies chorus line, etc. A limited edition, signed by Pogany, was published, but personalized inscribed copies of the trade edition, like the one included in this exhibition, are uncommon. (NY: E. P. Dutton, 1929; first edition.)

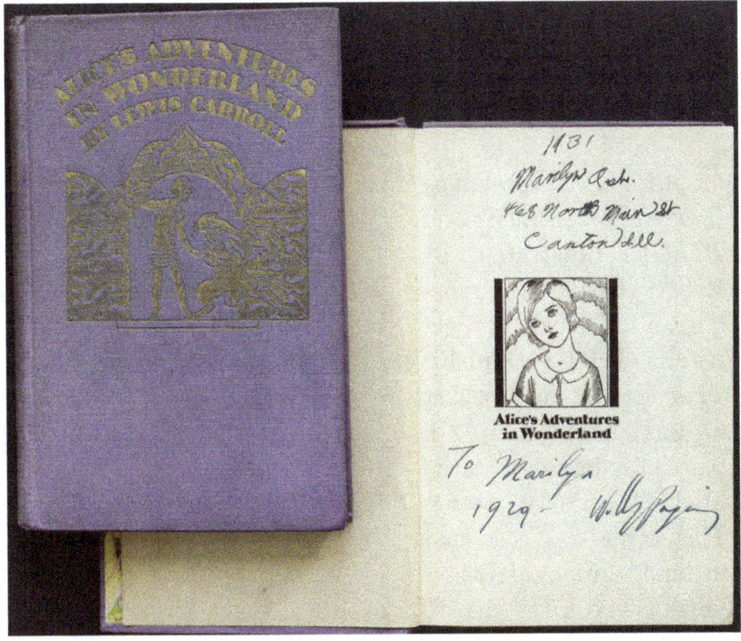

47   *L'Aventure Merveilleuse d'Alice* [*AAIW*]. Illustrated by Harry Rountree (1878–1950; New Zealander). Rountree's

marvelous *Alice*, first published in 1908 by Nelson (London), is the first *Alice* with a "down under" connection. His attention to facial expressions gives a fullness to his characters that is frequently lacking in many other editions. (London: Èdimbourg and NY: Nelson, *Éditeurs*, ca. 1915.)

48   *Alice's Adventures in Wonderland.* Illustrated by Milo Winter (1888–1956; American). Winter's illustrations were first published in 1916 by Rand McNally (Chicago). The quaint, scarce edition in this exhibition was published [ca. 1920–40] by Northern Paper Mills in Green Bay, Wisconsin, possibly an advertising give-away.

49   *Alices Äventyr i Sagolandet och Bakom Spegeln* [*AAIW and TTLG*]. Humorously illustrated by Robert Högfeldt (1894–1986; Swedish). Translated into Swedish by Gösta Knutsson (1908–1973; Swedish). Knutson was also a highly esteemed author and the asteroid "8534 Knutsson" was named by Uppsala astronomers in his honor. (Stockholm: Jan Förlag, 1945; first Swedish edition of the Högfeldt illustrations.)

50   *Alice i Æventyrland og Bag Spejlet* [*AAIW* and *TTLG*]. Illustrated by Robert Högfeldt. Translated into Danish by Kjeld Elfelt (1903–; Danish). The pictorial dust jacket for this edition has a pig in place of a dormouse in the Mad Tea-Party scene. This error was corrected in later editions. (København: Thorkild Becks, 1946; first Danish edition of the Högfeldt illustrations.)

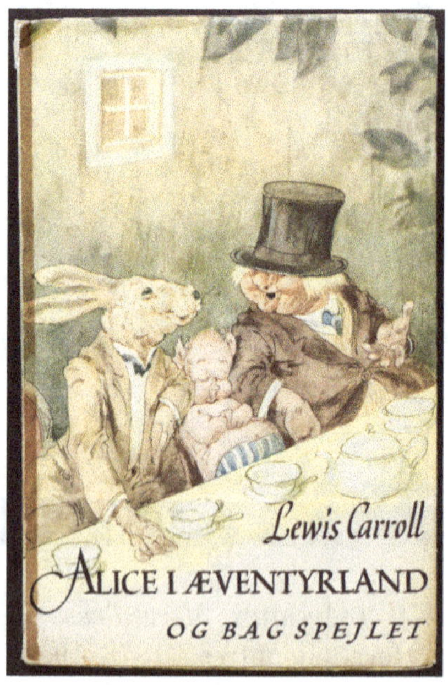

51 *Alice's Adventures in Wonderland and Through the Looking-Glass.* Illustrated by Mervyn Peake (1911–1968; English). Peake was born in China to missionary parents and lived in China for most of his boyhood; he resettled in England. This first edition was published in Sweden (due to a paper shortage in England after WWII) with English text. Charles Lovett (1962–; American) nicely describes some of these superb illustrations as having such characters as an offended and egocentric mouse, an enormously fat Duchess, and a hauntingly maniacal Cheshire Cat; the black and white drawings lend an air of grotesqueness to the book and walk a fine line between nightmare and nonsense. (Stockholm and London: The Continental Book Company, 1946; first edition.)

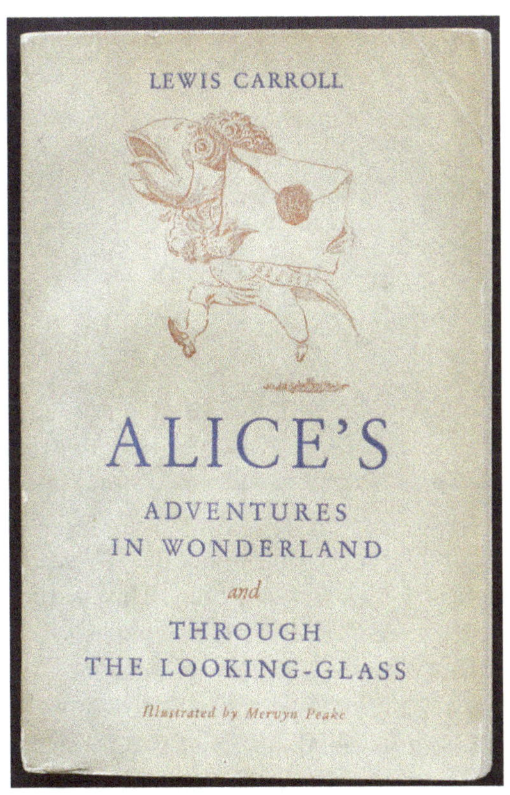

52   ふしぎの国のアリス. [*Fushigi no Kuni no Arisu; Arisu in Wonderland; AAIW*]. Masao Kusuyama, trans. Goro [later changed to Chikabo] Kumada, illus. (1911–2009; Japanese) No. 9 in the series "Complete Works of World Literature". Kumada is probably best known for his botanical and insect illustrations. His distinctive style is evidenced throughout this edition of *Alice*, even though they are all printed in black and white. (Tokyo: Kosansha, 1950; possibly a later printing).

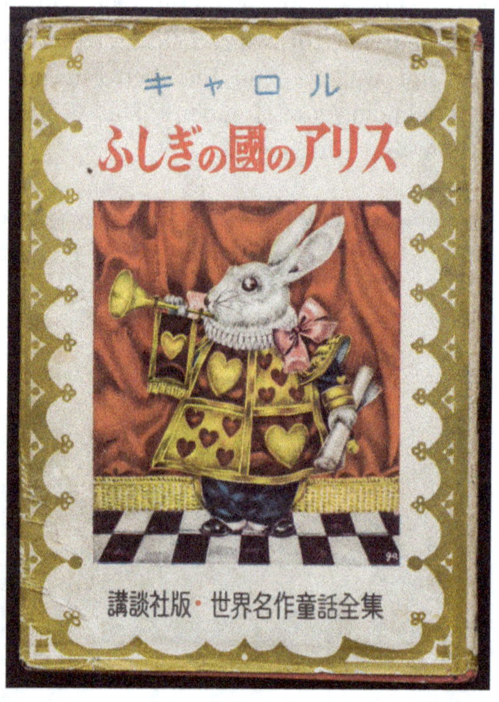

53   *Alice's Adventures in Wonderland and Through the Looking-Glass.* Illustrated by Mervyn Peake. This is the first Peake edition of *Alice and Looking-Glass* published in England. (London: Allan Wingate, 1954.)

54   *Alice's Adventures in Wonderland and Through the Looking-Glass.* Illustrated by Philip Gough (English). Gough was originally a London stage designer, but after WWII he focused

instead on book illustration. His rococo illustrations of *Alice* give a view of Wonderland seen nowhere else. Dressed in period costume, Alice appears closer to 30 years old than seven. Most of the period costumes and settings do not seem to fit the text and Gough stood virtually alone at the time in setting *Alice* in a pre-Victorian period. (London: The Heirloom Library, 1949.)

55–56 (55): *The Aventures of Alys in Wondyr Lond* [*AAIW*]. Translated into Middle English verse by Brian S. Lee (?–; South African). Illustrated in a Tennielesque style by Byron W. Sewell, in which the familiar characters are costumed in Chaucer-era (ca. 1340–1400) medieval attire. (Cathair na Mart: Evertype, 2013).

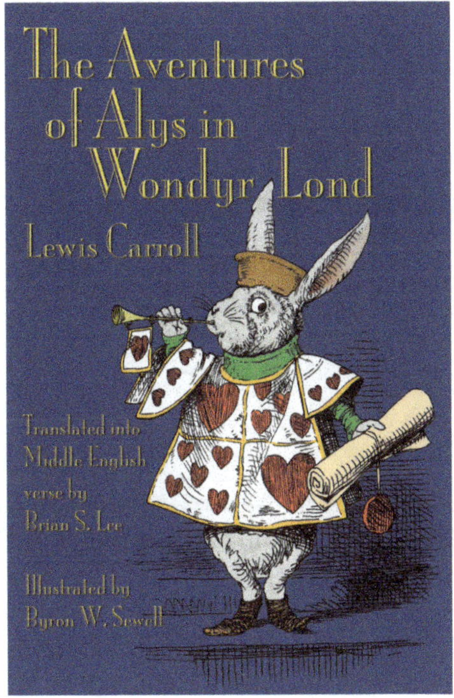

(56): Original art for Chapter IX, "The Mokke Se-Tortuses Tale" [equivalent to "The Mock Turtle's Story"), by Byron W. Sewell. Pen and ink on tracing paper vellum. 2011. In this illustration, based on Tenniel's original composition, Alys is holding a swan instead of the familiar flamingo.

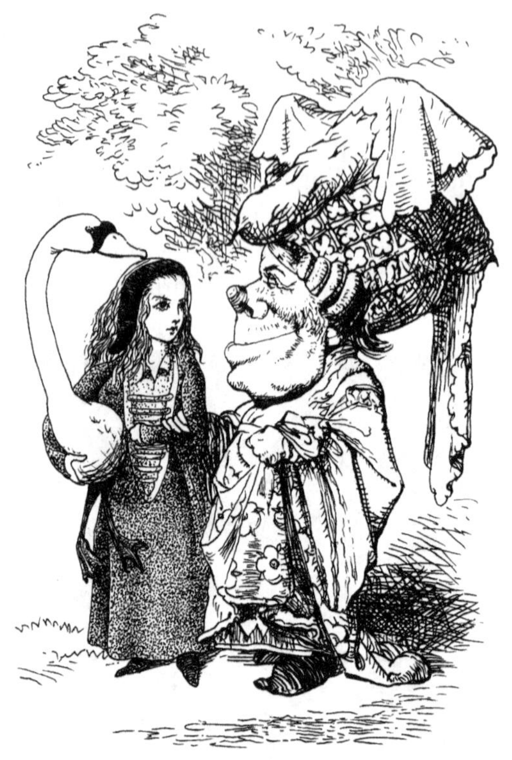

57   *Alice's Adventures in Wonderland.* Illustrated by [Libico] Maraja (1912–1983; Italian). (NY: Grosset & Dunlap, 1986 reprinting of the original 1957 edition.)

58   愛麗斯夢遊仙境 (*Àilìsī mèngyóu xiānjìng*; *Alice in Wonderland*). Translated into Chinese by Muyun Huang. Illustrated by Paiyi Chen. The front wrapper depicts a young Chinese *Alice* dressed in a red and white polka dot dress and wearing red shoes. The cover design combines several scenes (Alice racing after the White Rabbit; a giant Alice having grown

large in the long hall of doors; Alice passing through the small door into the garden; Alice racing to the White Rabbit's house). The White Rabbit reveals a strong influence from the Disney cinema version, but the remaining characters are quite original and the illustrations are intriguingly Chinese in style. (Hong Kong: Er Tong Le Yuan Ban Yue Kan, 1958; second printing.)

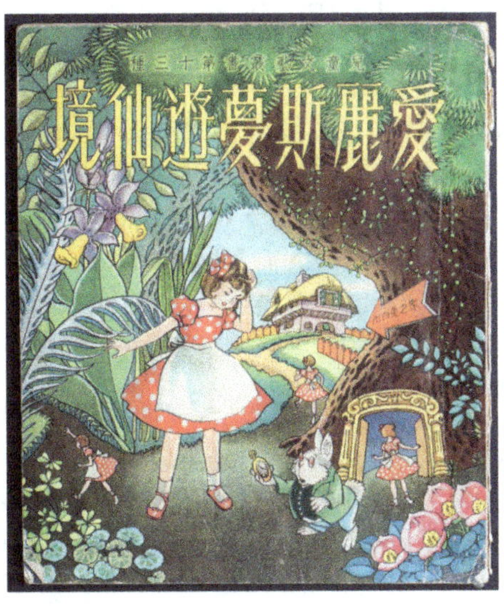

59   *The Annotated Alice.* Introduction, notes and bibliography by Martin Gardner. This book almost single-handedly sparked a renaissance in Lewis Carroll studies, which has continued to this day. The copy on display in this exhibition is the first edition (NY: Clarkson N. Potter, 1960) and is signed by Gardner. Gardner never stopped updating, publishing *More Annotated Alice* (NY: Random House, 1990) and *The Annotated Alice: The Definitive Edition* (NY: W. W. Norton, in 1999). This fall W. W. Norton will publish *The Annotated Alice: 150th Anniversary Deluxe Edition*, further updated and graced with 100 additional illustrations, under the editorship and art direction of LCSNA president emeritus Mark Burstein.

60   *Alice im Wunderland / Alice hinter den Spiegeln / Die Jagd nach dem Schnark [AAIW / TTLG / The Hunting of the Snark].* Illustrated by Ralph Steadman (1936 –; English). Steadman's outrageous illustrations for *Alice* were first published in 1967 (London: Denis Dobson) and for *Looking-Glass* in 1972 (London: MacGibbon & Kee). To Carroll's parody of Victorian England, Steadman answered with his own parody of modern England. Steadman's *Alice* is one of the most original ever created. The edition exhibited here is translated into German by Christian Enzensberger (1931–2009; German) and Klaus Reichert (1938–; German). From 1969 until 1982, Enzensberger was Professor of English Literature at the Ludwig Maximilian University of Munich. He is today chiefly known in Germany for his 1963 translation of *Alice* and *Looking-Glass*. Reichert is Professor of English and American studies at the Goethe University Frankfurt. (Hamburg: Zinnober Verlag, 1987).

61   *The Wasp in a Wig / A "Suppressed" Episode of Through the Looking-Glass and What Alice Found There.* Preface, introduction and notes by Martin Gardner. This is the first publication of this suppressed episode from *Looking-Glass* for the general public; an earlier edition was published for members of the Lewis Carroll Society of North America. This episode was already typeset in galleys, but Tenniel suggested that if Carroll wished to shorten the book, this part should be eliminated. Tenniel was famously said to have complained that it was impossible to illustrate a wasp in a wig. For many years the galleys were thought to have been destroyed, until in 1974 they were offered at auction in London and bought by Norman Armour, Jr., an American collector. They were published in various editions; the one exhibited here is the first American trade edition (NY: Clarkson N. Potter, 1977; signed by Gardner).

62   ふしぎの国のアリス [*Fushigi no Kuni no Arisu; Arisu in Wonderland; AAIW*]. Translated into Japanese by Yuka

Murayama. Illustrated by Tove Jansson (1914–2001; Finnish). Jansson was the recipient of the Hans Christian Anderson Award in 1966, the same year her illustrations for *Alice* were first published in Sweden (*Liisan saikkailut ihmemaasa*; WSOY). Her illustrations are at once imaginative and eerie, depicting a gothic, nightmarish side of Wonderland. (Tokyo: Media Factory, 2006). Jansson had previously illustrated Carroll's epic nonsense poem, *The Hunting of the Snark*. (*Snarkjakten*; Bonnier, 1959.)

63   *Alenka v kraji divů a Za zrcadlem* [*AAIW and TTLG*]. Illustrated by Markéta Prachatická (Czech). Translated into Czech by Hana Skoumalová (1903–1999; Czech). Prachatická's illustrations for *Alice* won her the prestigious Premio Grafico prize at the Bologna Children's Book Fair, the world's leading professional fair for children's books. (Praze: Albatros, 1985.)

64   *An, Sun-Hee's Adventures Under the Land of Morning Calm*. Adapted and illustrated by Victoria Sewell (1956–; American [West Virginia native]) and Byron Sewell (1942–; American). The main text is in English, with the Korean text in a separate small pamphlet that is loosely inserted in the book.

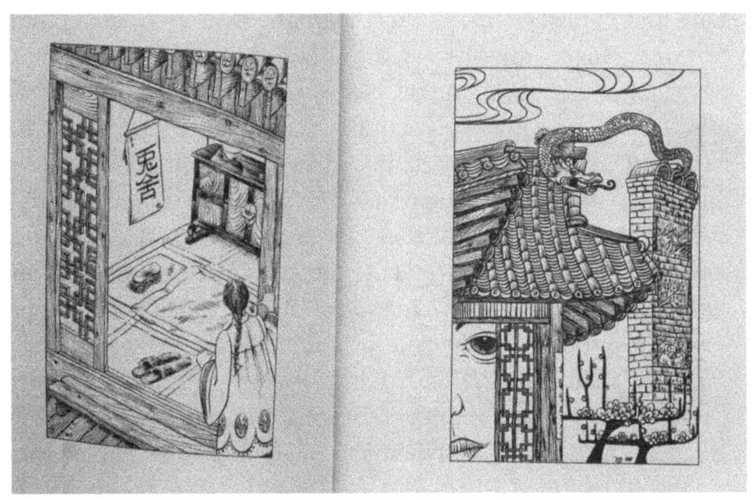

Another set reverses this, with the main text in Korean and the English text in a separate small pamphlet that is loosely inserted in the book. The Sewells lived in the Republic of Korea (South Korea) in 1984–85. The book is opened at pages 32–33. The illustration on the right, by Victoria Sewell, depicts a gigantic An, Sun-Hee (the Alice equivalent, whose name roughly translates as "fairyland girl") inside the White Rabbit's house. A small dragon (equivalent to Bill the Lizard) is seen exiting an ancient-style chimney, which was typically offset from the house a short distance as a precaution against fire. The stylized blossoming tree at the bottom is a design common on Korean-style playing cards. (Seoul: Sharing Place, 1990; first edition.)

65   *Alice au pays des merveilles* [*AAIW*]. Illustrated by Alain Gauthier (1931–; French). Translated by Jacques Papy. Some of Gauthier's surrealistic and dreamlike illustrations have been compared to those by surrealist painter Paul Delvaux (1897–1994; Belgian) and painter Balthus (born Balthasar Klossowski de Rola; 1908–2001; Polish-French). There is a distinctly erotic undercurrent in some of them. (Paris: Rageot Editeur, 1991.)

66–67 (66): *Alice's Adventures in Wonderland*. Illustrated by Barry Moser (1940–; American). Moser's illustrations for *Alice* were first published in 1992 by the Pennyroyal Press in a limited edition. Moser illustrated the *Alice* books primarily with portraits of real or historical people for the various characters. Similar to Peake and Jansson, his dark woodcuts bring out the haunting side of Wonderland, where the characters have a uniformly menacing, dangerous and maniacal quality that is disturbing, even though they are masterfully and elegantly rendered in the woodcuts. His vignettes in the margins and elsewhere allude to the opulence of Alice Liddell's own upper class background and help to brighten the otherwise pervasive darkness. The copy exhibited is the trade edition. (NY, San Diego, and London: Harcourt Brace Jovanovitch, 1982.) (67): "Lewis Carroll". A woodcut by Barry Moser, signed and numbered by him. 2013.

68   *Alice im Wunderland.* Illustrated by Jassen Ghiuselev (1964–; Bulgarian). Translated into German by Barbara Frischmuth (1941–; Austrian). Ghiuselev's illustrations are inspired by the Renaissance and 19th century English realism. This edition includes an elaborate fold-out loosely inserted at the back, which depicts the entire story of *Alice* in a single poster-size panel. (Berlin: Aufbau-Verlag, 2000; first edition). These same illustrations were also published in a traditional book. (Simply Read Books, 2003.)

69   *Alice in Wonderland.* Illustrated by Pat Andrea (1942–; Dutch). Translated by John Sillevis (1946–; Dutch). This bilingual Dutch-English catalogue was for an exhibition of Andrea's paintings at the Gemeentmuseum Den Hag in 2008. Many of his paintings are either risqué or pornographic, depending upon the viewer's sensitivities. (Harderwijk, Netherlands: de Jonge Hond, 2008.)

70   *Alice's Adventures in Wonderland.* Illustrated by Maggie Taylor (1961–; American). Taylor produces each print by scanning objects into a computer, then layering and manipulating these images using Photoshop into a seamless surrealistic montage. (Palo Alto, CA: Modernbook Editions, June 2008.) The HMoA has previously exhibited some of Taylor's work.

71   Οι Περιπέτειες της Αλίκης στη Χώρα των Θαυμάτωων (*Oi Peripéteies tēs Alíkēs stē Chóra tōn Thaumátōn; AAIW*). Illustrated by Robert Ingpen (1936–; Australian). Translated into Greek by Maria (unknown surname). Ingpen's illustrations were first published in 2009 (NY: Sterling). Ingpen received the biennial, international Hans Christian Andersen Medal in 1986. (Athens: Pataki, 2009.)

72–73 (72): *Alice's Adventures in Wonderland.* Illustrated by Oleg Lipchenko (1957–; Ukrainian). English text. Lipchenko, now resident in Toronto, Canada, was the winner of the 2009 Elizabeth Mrazik-Cleaver Canadian Picture Book Award for this edition of *Alice*. (NY: Tundra Books, 2009; trade edition). At this writing Lipchenko is busily illustrating an edition of *Looking-Glass*. He has also illustrated an edition of Carroll's *The Hunting of the Snark*. (NY: Tundra Books, 2012.) (73): "The Butcher". Orginal pencil illustration by Oleg Lipchenko prepared for his edition of *The Hunting of the Snark* published in 2010. However, this specific drawing was not included in the published edition.

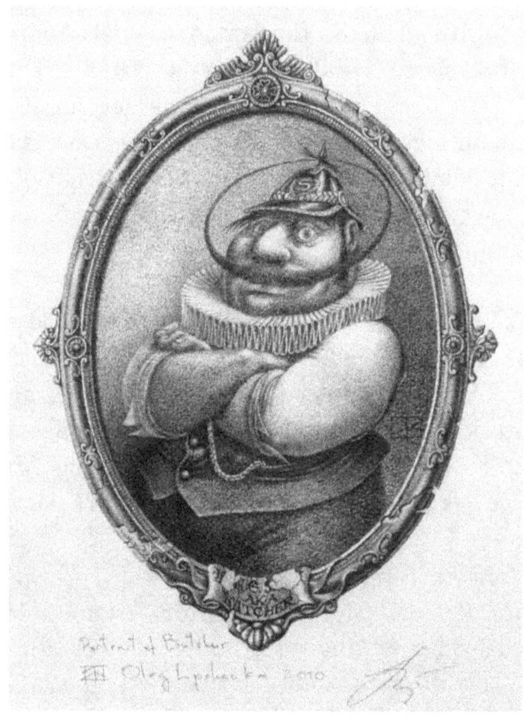

74   *Alicia en el País de las Maravillas* [*AAIW*]. Illustrated by Rébecca Dautremer (1971–; French). Translated into Spanish by Elena Gallo Krahe. This is the Spanish version of the original French edition published by Hachette in 2010. This magnificently illustrated oversize book is filled with very original and imaginative interpretations of *Alice*. (Madrid: Edelvives, 2012.)

75   *Alice in Wonderland*. Illustrated by Manuela Adreani (Italian). This oversize edition is magnificently illustrated with numerous double-page spreads in a very original style. She was one of the winners in a contest organized for the 130th anniversary of the creation of Pinocchio. (Novara, Italy: VBM, 2013.)

76   不思議の国のアリス [*Fushigi no Kuni no Arisu; AAIW*]. Illustrated by Yayoi Kusama (1929–; Japanese) in her iconic polka-dot style. An English edition of this book appeared first (Penguin Global, 2010). It was finally translated into Japanese in 2013 by Kimie Kusumoto, a prominent Japanese Carrollian. Sophie Knight, writing in a September 1, 2014 article in the *London Telegraph* (on-line edition), says of her: "At 85 Kusama is one of the art world's *grandes dames*, and also one of its great eccentrics. After making a name for herself in New York in the 1960s as a renegade…she retreated to cope with her mental illness and returned to Japan, which did not initially embrace its taboo-busting prodigal daughter. But in the past 15 or so years Kusama has been granted a critical reassessment with recent retrospectives propelling her back into the limelight." It seems unlikely that she did these illustrations specifically for *Alice*, but rather that they were selected by the book's Japanese editor, Tatako Motoki, because they alluded to the text in some (often obscure) way. (Tokyo: Graphic-sha, 2013; first Japanese edition; this copy is inscribed by Kusumoto.)

77   *Alice in Blunderland / An Iridescent Dream*. John Kendrick Bangs (1862–1922; American). Illustrated by Albert Levering (1869–1929). This political parody is critical of economic issues such as taxation, corporate greed, and corruption. Instead of entering Wonderland, Alice finds herself in "Blunderland", which is also described as "Municipal Ownership Country". The illustration below is for Chapter III, "The Aromatic Gas Plant". (NY: Doubleday, Page, 1907; first edition.)

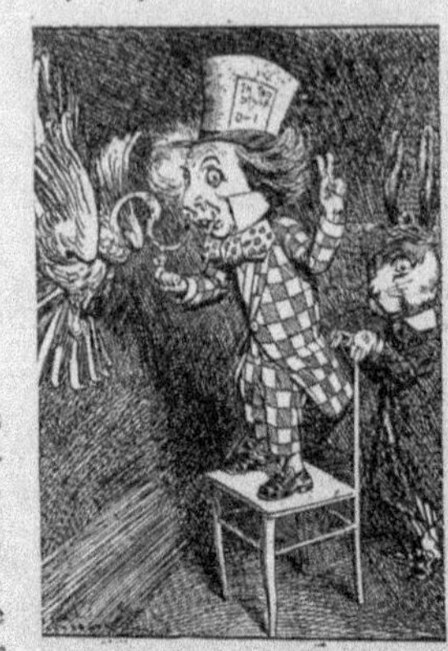

"NOBODY COULD BE GAS-FIXTURATED"

78   *Malice in Kulturland*. Horace Wyatt (1876–1954; English).
Illustrated by W. Tell. This WWI political parody (British
propaganda) caricatures Franz Joseph (Emperor of Austria)
and Kaiser Wilhelm II, who is lampooned as the "Kaiserhog",
the equivalent of the Jabberwock. (London: "The Car
Illustrated", 1915; reprint of the 1904 first ed.). Wyatt had
previously authored *Alice in Motorland* (1904).

79   *Uncle Wiggly and Alice in Wonderland*. Howard R. Garis
(1873–1962; American). Illustrated by Edward Bloomfield.
This is one in the series of books featuring Uncle Wiggly
Longears, an elderly rabbit with rheumatism who walks with the
assistance of a candy-striped cane. The first Uncle Wiggly story
appeared in 1910. Ultimately, Garis wrote an astonishing
15,000 Uncle Wiggly stories, though most of these appeared
weekly in newspapers. This is not a true parody, and is perhaps

better understood as a pastiche with some *Alice* characters. (Chicago and NY: M. A. Donohue, 1918.)

80   *Mr. Tompkins in Wonderland or Stories of c, G, and h.* George Gamow (1904–1968; Russian). Illustrated by John Hookham. Gamow was a theoretical physicist, cosmologist and early advocate of the "Big Bang" theory about the creation of the universe. He was awarded the Kalinga Prize by UNESCO for his work in popularizing science, noting especially *Mr. Tompkins.* This copy is inscribed by Gamow as: "To the Scient. Adv. Comm. of the Army Air Force this non-confidential document is confidentially presented. / G. Gamow / Apr. 1945." (Cambridge: At the University Press, 1939.) Gamow is probably referring to "the Scientific Advisory Commission of the Army Air Force", or some such similar governmental jargon.

81   *Alice Through the Paper-mill.* Arthur Wragg (1903–1976; British), author and illustrator. In one of the book's splendid black and white illustrations we find Alice smoking a cigarette, which might well be a first.

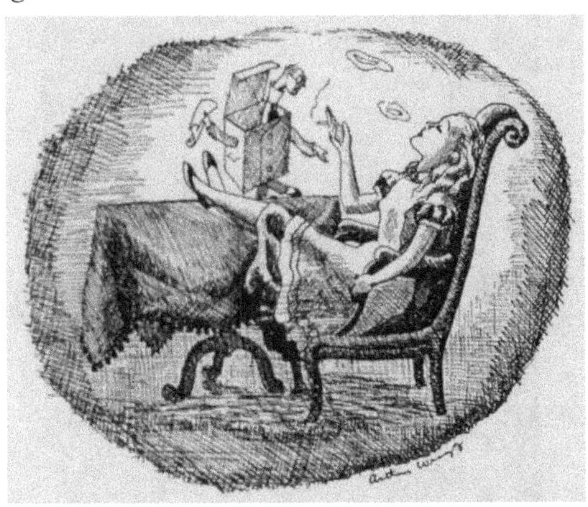

Wragg was a socialist and pacifist, who was imprisoned during WWII as a conscientious objector. (Birmingham: C. F. Foyle, Boxfoldia Ltd., [1940]; second edition.)

82   *Alice's Adventures in Atomland in the Plastic Age / A Stark Fantasy by Daddy Dumps alias Humpty Dumpty, alias Deadeye Dick.* Richard M. Field. (Duxbury, MA: Faulkner & Field, 1949; first edition; signed by Field). In the opinion of Byron Sewell, this is the best cover of an *Alice* parody ever published. It also features some first rate parodies of *Alice* poetry. Here is a typical example, this a parody of "*Twinkle, Twinkle Little Bat*":

> *"Faster, faster, little plane!*
> *How I wonder what your gain!*
> *Up above the world so high,*
> *Like a meteor in the sky.*
> *First you devastate Japan,*
> *Now we wonder what's your plan?*
> *Will you atomize the moon,*
> *Or try to colonize Neptune?"*

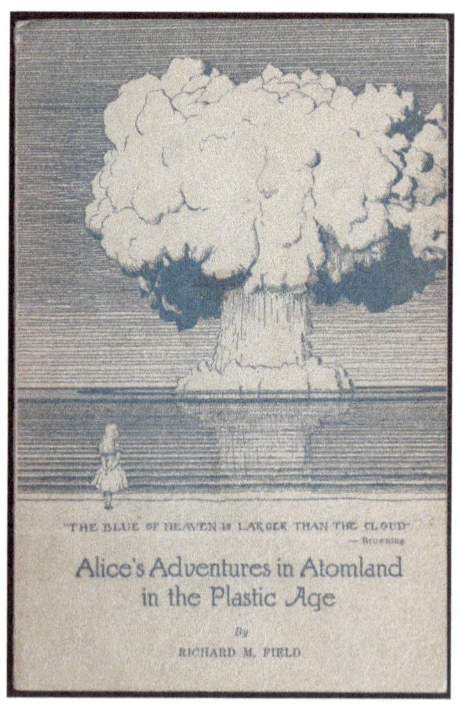

83   *The Pogo Stepmother Goose.* Walt Kelly (1913–1973), cartoonist and author. Included in this collection is "A Report from Lewis Carroll's *Alice's Adventures in Wonderland* / Who Stole the Tarts?" In this marvelously illustrated cartoon-style version of the Trial Scene from *Alice,* the famous cartoon strip's main characters assume the various roles, with Pogo Possum taking the lead role of Alice. Others include: Albert Alligator as The Gryphon; Easter Bun as the White Rabbit; Bun Rabbit as the March Hare; Mamselle Hepzibah as the Dormouse; Deacon Mushrat as The Queen; Beauregard Bugleboy as the Hatter; Beaver as The Dutchess' Cook; and, Simple J. Malarkey as the King. Great fun and highly recommended! (NY: Simon and Schuster, 1954; first printing.)

84   *The Campaign Alice or Through the Election Booth & How She Lost Her Innocence.* Jim Quinn, author. Illustrated by Mike Kanarek. A humorless, rude, and mean-spirited adult political parody about President Richard Nixon's reelection bid. (Philadelphia, PA: Mixed Media, 1971).

85   *Witch Hill / A History of Salem Witchcraft.* Rev. Z. A. Mudge, author. The spine of this book is perhaps the earliest pirated use of a John Tenniel illustration (redrawn) from *Alice.* In the middle of the spine one sees Alice in the Duchess's kitchen, where a grinning Cheshire Cat can be seen warming itself by the stove. The implication seems to be that Alice is a young witch and the cat is her familiar. There is little doubt that Dodgson would have refused permission to use the image of his Wonderland characters in this way. (NY: Nelson & Phillips / Cincinnati: Hitchcock & Walden, 1871).

86–87 (86): *Another Alice, Eh?* Byron W. Sewell, author and illustrator. This parody of *Alice* is set in Banff National Park in Alberta and lampoons some of Canada's contemporary politicians. In the first illustration (below) is satirized The Right Honourable Sir Wilfred Laurier (1841–1919, the Seventh Prime Minister of Canada (1896–1911), who was involved in the creation of the Yukon Territory, Saskatchewan and Alberta (the provincial setting of the parody). Laurier's portrait graces the blue Canadian five dollar bill, the traditional color of the Caterpillar in *Alice*. This parody was published for The Lewis Carroll Society of Canada. (Shelburne, ON, Canada: The Battered Silicon Dispatch Box, 2002.) (87): An original illustrations from *Another Alice, Eh?* by Byron W. Sewell. Pen and ink on drafting vellum. 1999. In the parody the mad croquet scene has been transplanted into a mad game of golf. Here the King of Hearts is confronted by a grizzly bear that has wandered onto the links. The Sewells resided in Calgary from 1998–2000.

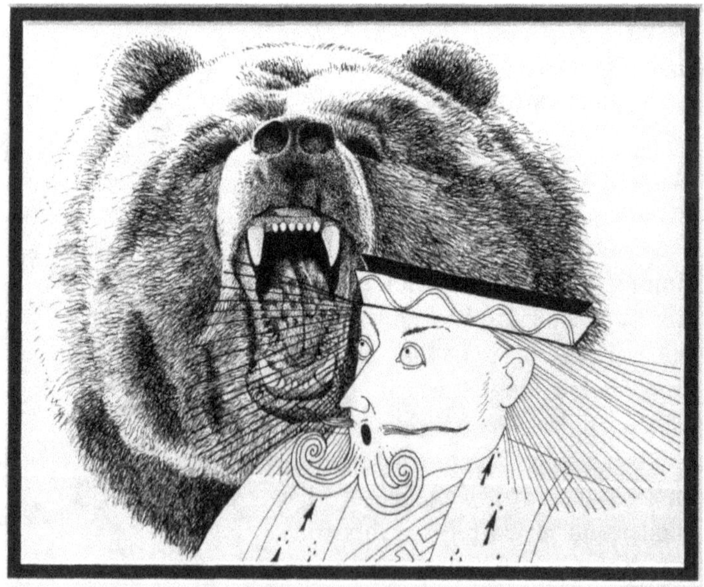

88   *Adolf in Blunderland*. James Dyrenforth (1895–1973) and Max Kester, authors. Illustrated by Norman Mansbridge (1911–1993; British). This WWII political parody lampoons Adolf Hitler as a young boy dressed up like Little Lord Fauntleroy (in place of Alice) and Neville Chamberlain as the Caterpillar. Mansbridge is most often remembered as a British cartoonist. Curiously, *Adolf in Blunderland* was recently reprinted in Germany (where it had never been published), requiring special permission due to strict German laws prohibiting publication of Nazi symbols. (Toronto: McClelland & Stewart, 1940; first Canadian edition.)

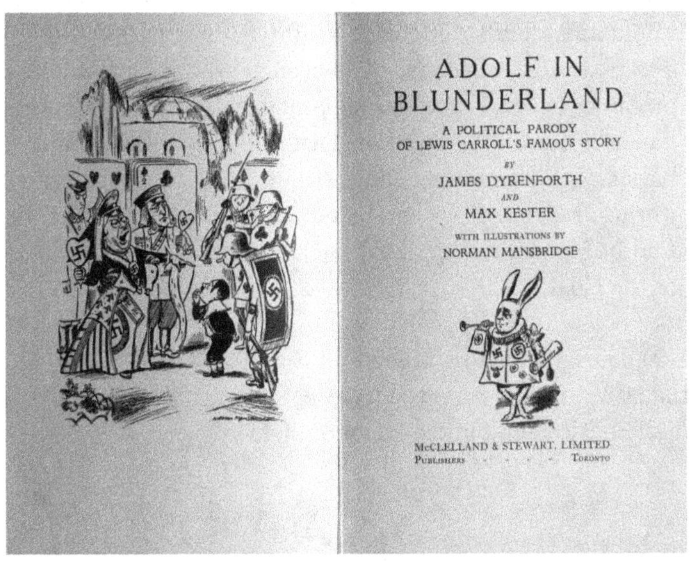

89–91 (89): *Álopk's Adventures in Goatland*. Byron Sewell. Illustrated by Mahendra Singh (1961–; US/CDN citizen). (Cathair na Mart: Evertype, 2011.) This pastiche, involving bits and pieces of an artificial language, is a bit complicated and best described by Sewell himself (in the tongue-in-cheek introduction) as follows:

Róaž Wiðz (1882–1937), the locally-admired though otherwise little-known Zumorgian translator, spent seventeen years of his miserable life (when he wasn't tending to his beloved goats) translating Lewis Carroll's classic *Alice's Adventures in Wonderland* into Zumorigénflit and transposing it into Ŋúǧian culture. Sadly, Ŋúǧ was swallowed up by the Soviet Union in 1947. For those interested in such esoteric things, *Áloþk üjy Gígið Soagénličy* was first published by the Itadabükan Press in the capital city of Sprutničovyurt in 1919. The city, which was mistakenly thought to be a German forward supply area, was literally flattened and burned to the ground by Royal Air Force saturation bombing in 1943, and all that remains of it are a few remnants of the ancient Palace's foundations and a gigantic reinforced concrete statue of Joseph Stalin, whose face has been shattered by what was probably machine gun target practice. The original story has here been updated to modern times, as if this strange, harsh, and dangerous land still existed in the modern world. It doesn't, except in Sewell's imagination and in that of Mahendra Singh, whose heart swells with the Song of the Goat.

(90–91): Original art by Mahendra Singh for Chapters IX and XI (the latter used also on the front cover) of *Áloþk's Adventures in Goatland*. Pen and ink on vellum. 2011.

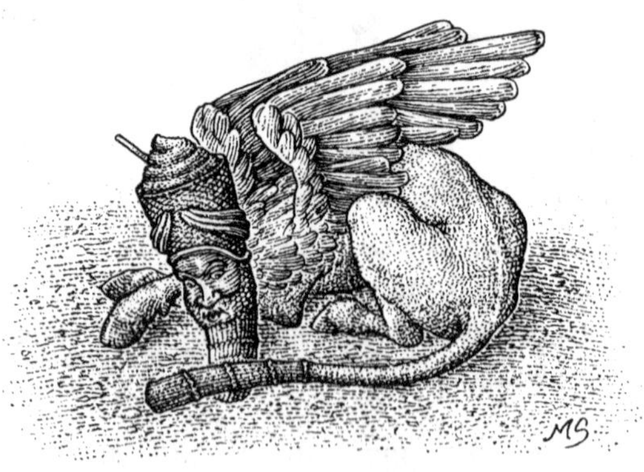

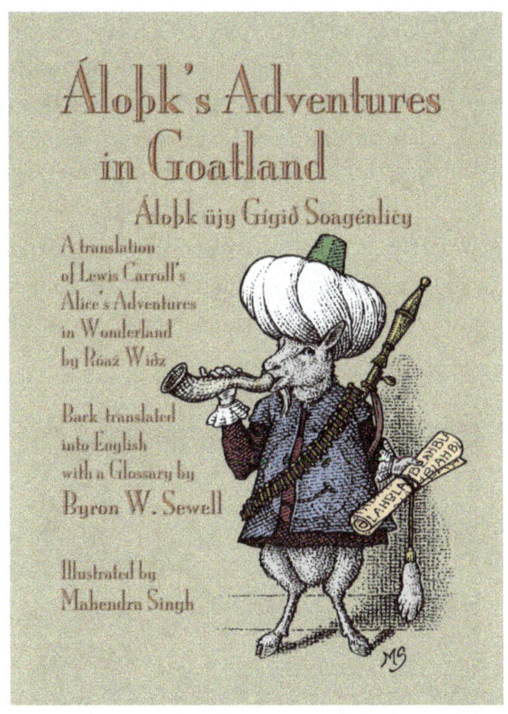

92 *Alice's Bad Hair Day in Wonderland / A Tangled Tale*. Byron W. Sewell, author and illustrator. Foreword by Stephanie [Stoffel] Lovett (1962–; American; currently the President of the LCSNA). In this retelling of Lewis Carroll's classic tale, Alice's fall down the rabbit hole turns into a terrifying descent through the center of the earth, accelerating her to terminal velocity, hopelessly snarling her long hair into a tangled mess, and nearly setting it alight. Things go from bad to worse as she sets out through Wonderland's familiar, yet strangely-altered places, where she encounters characters whose personalities have also radically changed. There is no timid mouse in the pool of tears she creates when weeping over the absolute mess of her hair, but rather a French sewer rat. Climbing out of the pool she encounters the last of the Dodos, the lonely, love-sick, sole survivor of his species, who ended up in Wonderland by diving down another hole, narrowly evading a starving, voracious

Dutch sailor. Travelling from place to place seeking a haircut (and at times, a shave), Alice also encounters the Queen of Hearts, who resembles an overweight Spanish beauty and who performs for Alice an energetic flamenco, leaving her Majesty too exhausted to play croquet. Instead of a Hatter, Alice meets a Hairdresser, and at one point has a close encounter of the worst kind with the Wasp from Looking-glass Land, who takes her for a tasty-looking larva. In the end, Alice's hair takes center stage in a surprising and hilarious climax. (Cathair na Mart: Evertype, 2011.)

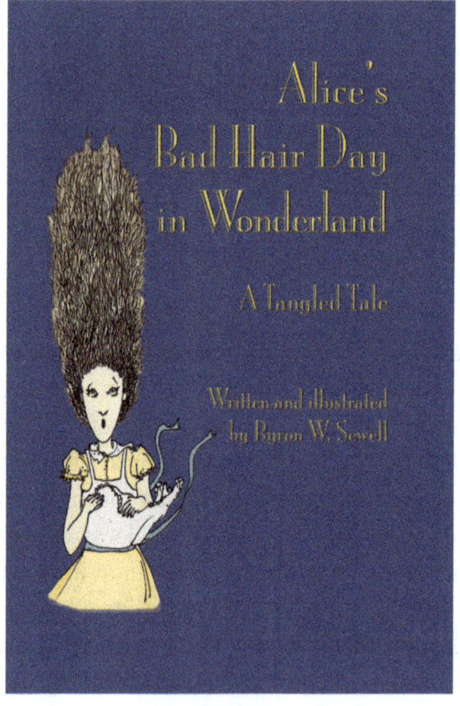

93–95 (93): *Alice's Adventures in an Appalachian Wonderland.* Byron W. Sewell and Victoria J. Sewell, authors. Illustrated after Tenniel, with minor exceptions, and foreword by Byron W. Sewell. Preface by August A. Imholtz, Jr. "On Dialect Orthography" by Michael Everson. This translation of *Alice* into the rich dialect of the Appalachian Mountains treats the story as a folktale, in order to create the sense that the reader is listening as an adult tells the story to a child. The story has been transported from Victorian English to post-Civil War West Virginia, into an Appalachian setting appropriate for the dialect. The spelling used aims towards a literary orthography, rather than towards a phonemic respelling of the language. The sounds of the language used in *Alice's Adventures in an Appalachian Wonderland* will certainly be familiar to most Appalachian readers, but a short glossary has also been included. Here Alice follows the White Rabbit into a coal mine shaft to Wonderland. (Cathair na Mart: Evertype, 2012.)

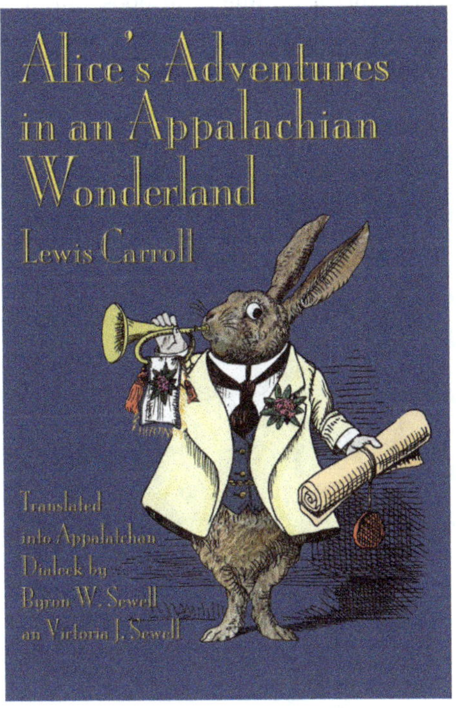

Two original illustrations for *Alice's Adventures in an Appalachian Wonderland* by Byron W. Sewell. Gel ink on parchment tracing paper. 2012. (94): In the first illustration, for

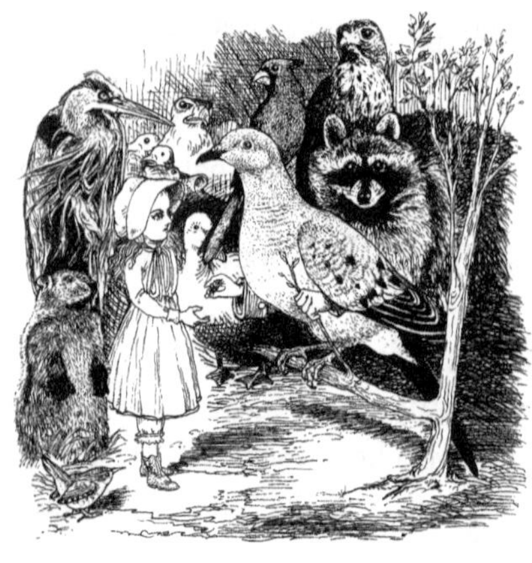

Chapter III, "A Cloggin Party an a Long Tale," Alice is surrounded by typical Appalachian animals and birds, about to receive her prize from a Passenger Pigeon, who like the Dodo in the original *Alice*, is now extinct. (95): In the second illustration, for Chapter VIII, "Play Ball!", the rhododendron blossoms (instead of roses) are being painted by three forest animals (an opossum, a raccoon, and a badger) instead of the original card-gardeners. In the parody the animals play baseball instead of croquet.

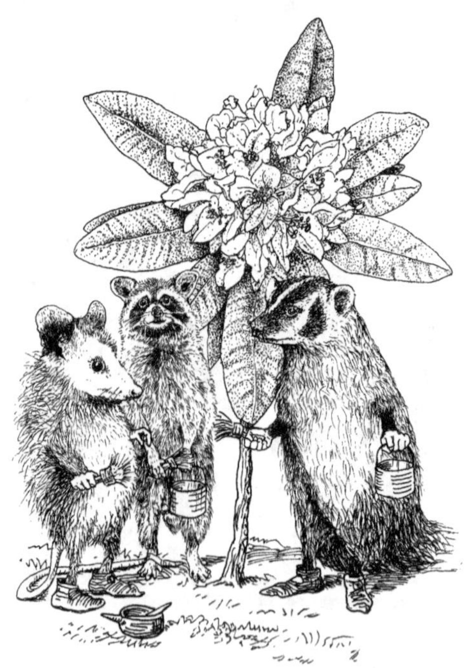

96   *Gods of Riverworld.* Philip José Farmer (1918–2009; American). This is the last volume in the fantasy/sci-fi "Riverworld" saga. Farmer won the 1972 Hugo Award for the first volume, *To Your Scattered Bodies Go.* A major character in several of the books is a repeatedly reincarnated Alice Pleasance Hargreaves. This final volume's pictorial dust jacket features a memorable Carrollian panorama of a furious battle between various characters in the books (including Sir Richard Burton and Alice Hargreaves) and some of Tenniel's literary versions that have implausibly come to life under the God-like power of Snark, the name of the super-computer that controls Riverworld. (NY: G. P. Putnam's Sons, 1983.)

97   "Mimsy Were the Borogoves." Lewis Padgett. Illustrated by Kolliker. *Astounding Science-Fiction*, Vol. XXX, No. 6, Feb. 1943. Lewis Padgett was the pseudonym of the married sci-fi writing team of Henry Kuttner (1915–1958; American) and Catherine Lucile Moore (1911–1987; American). This short story was later expanded and developed into the 2007 fantasy/sci-fi movie, *The Last Mimzy*, directed by Robert Slaye.

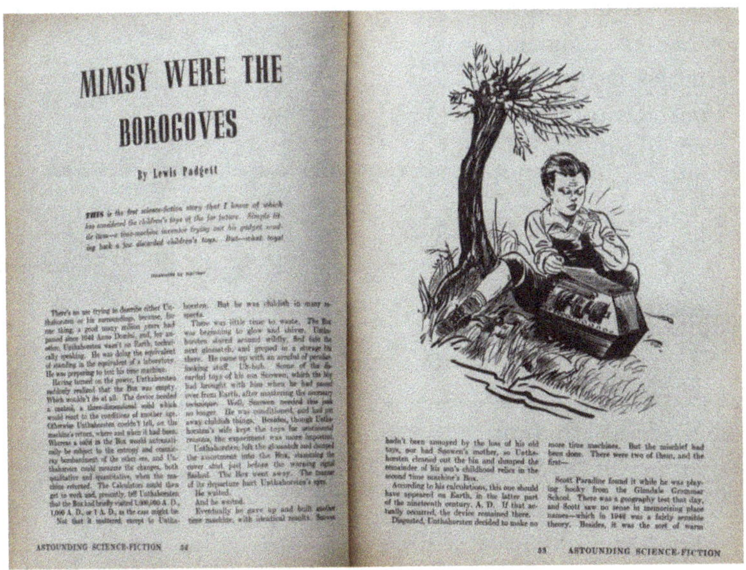

98–99 (98): *Alice's World*. Sam J. Lundwall (born Sam Thore Jerrie Lundwall; 1941–; Swedish). This classic sci-fi novel was first published in America (Ace, 1971). (99): Also exhibited here is the less familiar 1985 German edition, *Alices Welt*. The blurb tells the reader: "It is fifty thousand years since the Exodus. Fifty thousand years since the Empire deserted Earth for a new administrative centre among the stars. Now the spaceships are back, hovering warily above an unknown, almost legendary world. Man has returned to scavenge among the ruins of his abandoned home. But on the derelict surface of the planet, a chaos of dreams awaits. Pegasus glides softly on his mighty wings, the Sphinx repeats her deadly riddle—and a little golden-haired girl gazes thoughtfully towards the sky."

100 *Tennyson's Gift*. Lynne Truss (1955–; English). This delightful novel, arguably one of the funniest ever written, involves an imagined chaotic week in "Farringford", the Tennyson home overlooking Freshwater Bay on the Isle of Wight, in the summer of 1864. The cast of historical personages includes: Charles Dodgson; the Poet Laureate, Alfred, Lord Tennyson (1809–1892; English) and his wife Emily; their neighbor, the photographer, Julia Margaret Cameron (1815–1879; English); the painter, George Frederic Watts (1817–1904; English) and his new

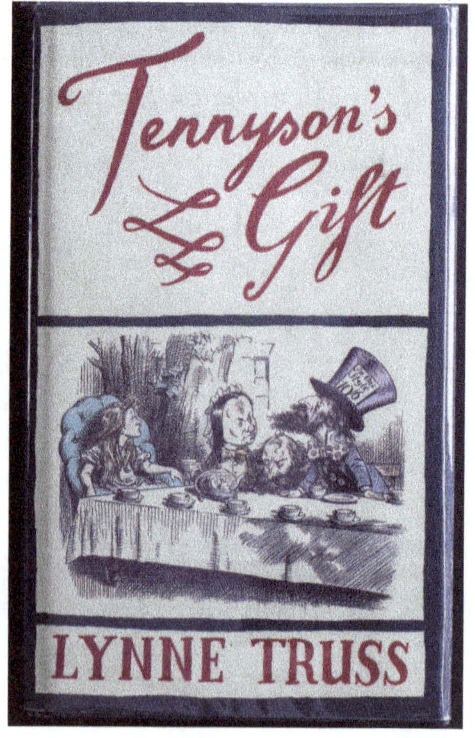

(much younger) wife, the Shakespearean actress Ellen Terry; and, Lorenzo [Niles] Fowler (1811–1896; American), the foremost American phrenologist. This copy is signed by Truss, who has written, "*Tennyson's Gift* is, of all my books, my darling, and I won't hear a word said against it." It is indeed a darling novel. (London: Hamish Hamilton, 1996; first edition.)

101 Ellen Terry (born Alice Ellen Terry; 1847–1928; English), costumed as Beatrice from Shakespeare's *Much Ado about Nothing.* [post-1882]. This is a Raphael Tuck, "Real Photograph postcard", by Window & Grove. Inscribed by Terry at the bottom

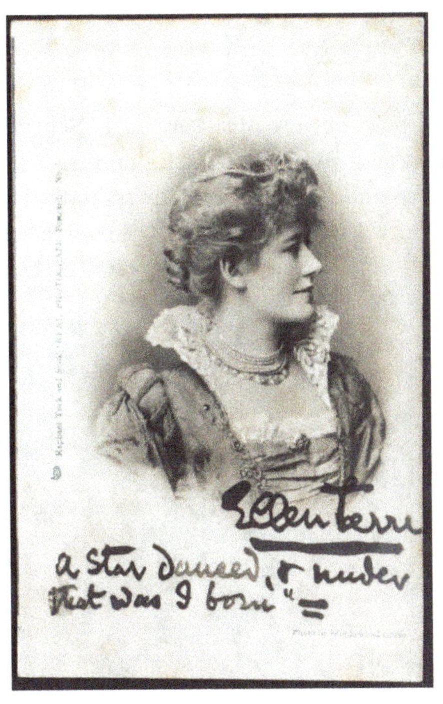

of the postcard as: *"Ellen Terry / a Star danced, & under that was I born"* = ". This is a quote from *Much Ado about Nothing*, Act 2, Scene 1, spoken by Beatrice to Don Pedro. The inference is that Terry believed that she qualified for this assessment. Many people who watched her performances agreed. She is often described as the greatest Shakespearian actresses of the Victorian era. Carroll was a close friend of the Terry family, including Ellen and her sister Kate, and photographed them.

102–103 (102): *Night of the Jabberwock.* Fredric Brown (1906–1972; American). This novel is based upon a short story that first appeared in the pulp magazine, *Thrilling Mystery*, Vol. XXII, No. 1, Summer Issue, 1944, a copy of which is included in this exhibition

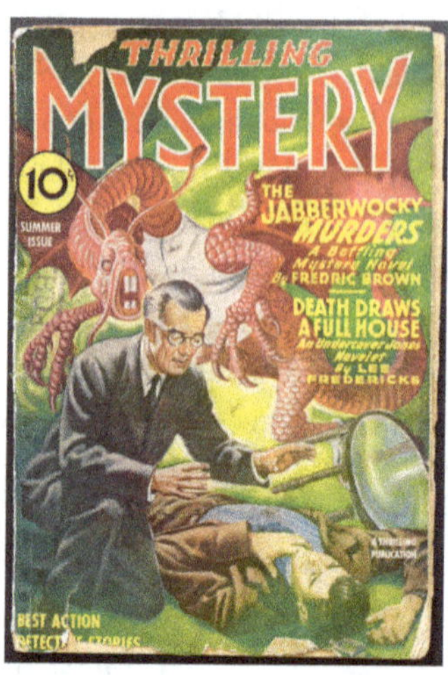

(103). The narrator is a very heavy drinker. Dr. Selwyn Goodacre, the world's preeminent authority on the minutiae of Carroll's revisions to the *Alice* and *Looking-Glass* texts, took the trouble to catalog how many alcoholic drinks the narrator consumed over the 12 hour span of the story. He concluded that it was the equivalent of three full bottles of whisky! (NY: E. P. Dutton, 1950; first edition, in an original dust jacket featuring a Tennielesque Jabberwock.) Some of Brown's other famous novels feature equally heavy drinkers, including *The Fabulous Clipjoint* (1947) and *The Screaming Mimi* (1949). Brown also penned a short story entitled "Death is a White Rabbit", published in *Strange Detective Mysteries* in January 1942.

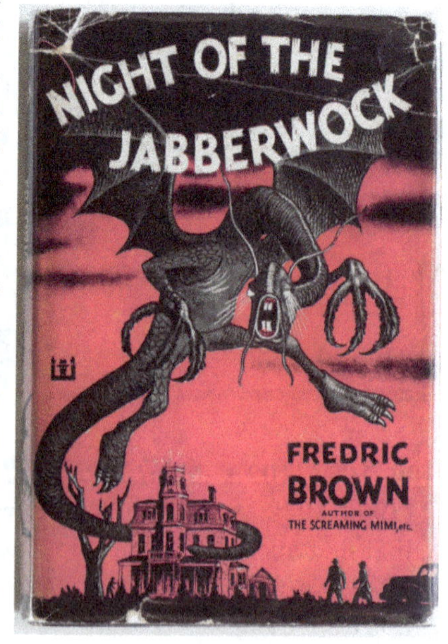

104–105 (104): *Murder in Wonderland.* George Bagby, pseudonym of Aaron Mark Stein (1906–1985; American). This mystery begins in NYC's Central Park at the iconic "Alice in Wonderland" statue. (London: Hammond, Hammond, 1965; first English edition.) (105): Also included in the exhibition is a copy of the American edition, published by Doubleday for The Crime Club, as *Mysteriouser and Mysteriouser,* a lovely pun on Alice's famous exclamation, "Curiouser and Curiouser!". The sketch for the dust jacket is based on the "Alice in Wonderland" statue in Central Park. (Garden City, NY: Doubleday, 1965; first American edition.)

106 This striking cover by Remy Charlip (1929–2012; American), is for a mystery short story anthology by Rufus King (1893–1966; American) published for The Crime Club. All of the stories are set in the fictional town of Halycon, Florida. Halycon is a common name for the kingfisher, used here as a pun on the author's surname. The first story, "Malice in Wonderland", features a young girl of nine named Alice Wickershield. It's difficult to see, but the palm fronds on the cover design are cut from a section of a roadmap for Palm Beach. These stories originally appeared in *The Saint Magazine* and *Ellery Queen's Mystery Magazine.* (Garden City, NY: Doubleday, 1958. First edition.)

107 *The Carrollian Tales of Inspector Spectre*. Byron W. Sewell and August A. Imholtz, Jr. (1943–; American), co-authors. Illustrated by Byron W. Sewell and Harry Furniss (1854–1925; Irish). Foreword by Edward Wakeling (1946–; British). This collection includes: a) *R. I. P. (Restless in Pieces)* by Byron Sewell (partly set in West Virginia, it predicts a future Lewis Carroll exhibition to be held at the HMoA, along with a Sewell drawing of the museum's main building); b) "What Happened to the Diaries" (a brilliant analysis by Edward Wakeling concluding with the likely identity of who destroyed several volumes of Carroll's *Diaries*); and, c) *The Oxfordic Oracle*, co-authored by Sewell and Imholtz, a humorous farce about the imagined inspiration for some of the "He thought he saw…" poems in Carroll's failed *Sylvie and Bruno* novels. (Cathair na Mart: Evertype, 2011.)

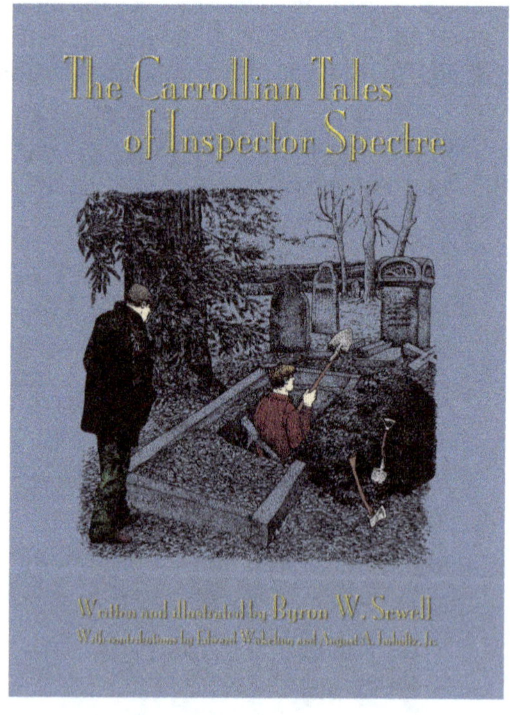

108   "Mr. H. Savile Clarke". This photograph appeared in *The Theatre. / A Monthly Review of The Drama, Music, and the Fine Arts*. London: Strand Publishing, 1889, "New Series", Vol. XIII, Jan – June 1889. In 1886 Savile Clarke (1841–1893; English), a minor dramatist and critic, sought permission from Carroll to stage *Alice* and *Looking-Glass* as a two act operetta. Dodgson quickly agreed and Savile Clarke chose Walter Slaughter (1860–1908) as the composer. The first performance occurred December 23, 1886 at The Prince of Wales' Theatre in London to largely favorable reviews. There are only a few surviving vintage copies of the original script.

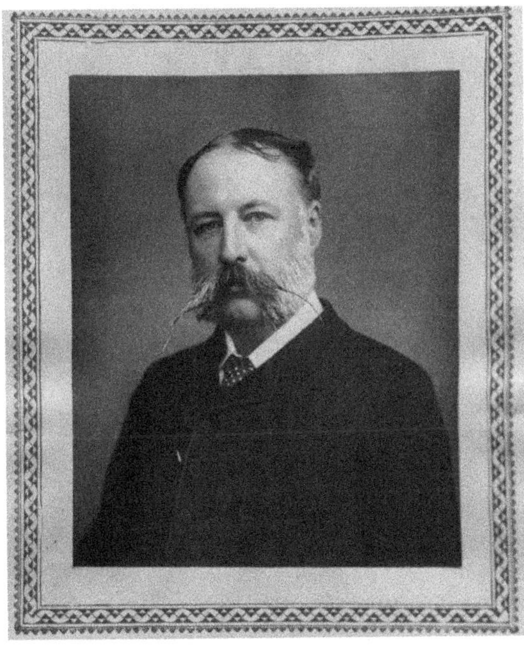

109   "Alice and the Dormouse". This photograph appeared in *The Theatre. / A Monthly Review of The Drama, Music, and the Fine Arts*. London: Strand Publishing, 1889, "New Series", Vol. IX, Jan – June 1887. Dodson proposed that his child-friend, Phoebe Carlo, be considered for the role of Alice and Savile Clarke

agreed, making her the first person to have performed the role of Alice on the legitimate stage.

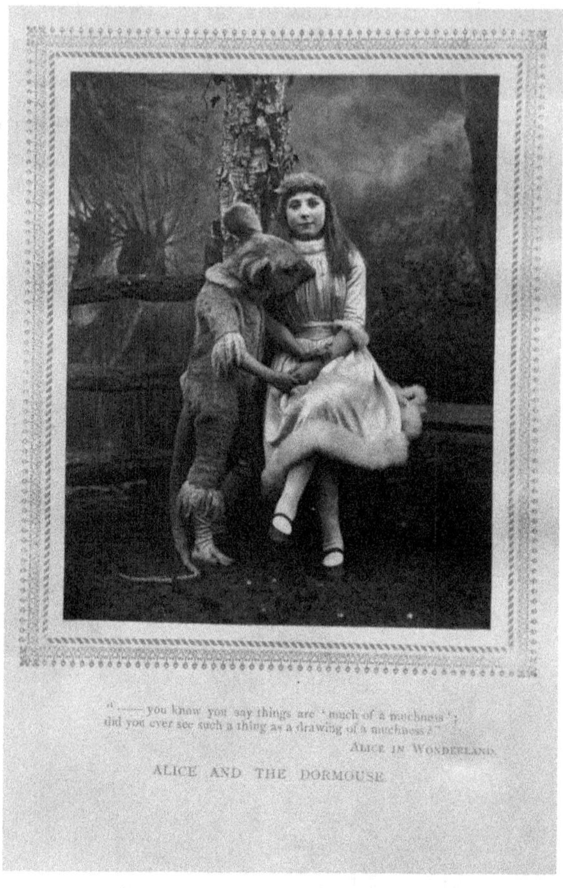

110 "London Christmas Pantomimes". This tear sheet, from the *Illustrated London News* for January 1888, discusses the 1886–87 performance of H. Savile Clarke's production of *Alice in Wonderland / A Dream Play for Children in Two Acts* at The Prince of Wales' Theatre. There are eight illustrations here of the play, four of which are based upon photographs by Elliot & Fry, London.

111–112 (111): At age twelve Mabel Love (1874–1953; English) played the part of The Rose in Savile Clarke's *Alice*. This tear sheet from *The Sketch* for October 4, 1893 depicts her as she looked when she was a few years older. (112) After Love's "discovery" in her role in *Alice* she went on to become one of the most beautiful and highly acclaimed dancers and actresses of the Edwardian era, and certainly one of the most photographed. Charles Lovett has described her as the equivalent of the "It-girl" of the Edwardian era. Early in her career she attempted suicide by casting herself into the Thames. A passing physician saw her jump and managed to rescue her. Winston Churchill is said to have written to her requesting an autographed photograph. Whether she obliged him is unknown.

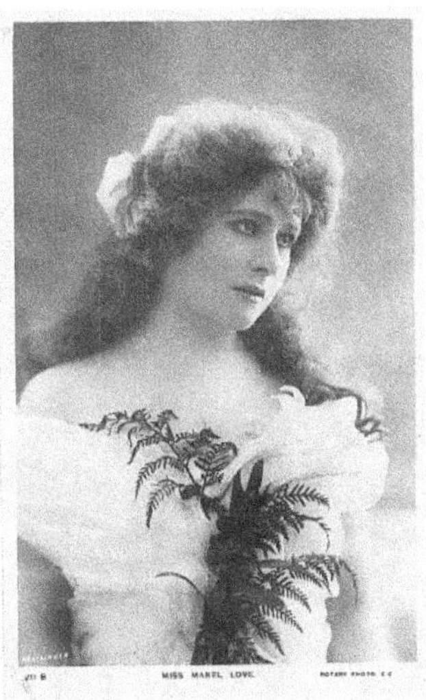

113–114 (113): English actress Isa Bowman (1874–1958) was chosen for the role of Alice in the 1889 revival of Savile Clarke's *Alice* operetta at the Royal Globe Theatre in London. Exhibited here is an original trifold program from a performance on the 5th of January 1889, just two weeks after the opening. (114): Isa Bowman met Carroll in 1886 when she had a minor role in one of Savile Clarke's performances of *Alice*. Bowman authored the memoir exhibited here about Carroll's life, strangely entitled *The Story of Lewis Carroll, Told for Young People by the Real Alice in Wonderland*, this in spite of the fact that she was no such thing. Carroll dedicated his failed novel, *Sylvie and Bruno* (NY and London: Macmillan, 1889) to her, including her name in a remarkable double acrostic prefatory poem. Curiously, she didn't recognize what he had done and Carroll had to eventually write to her and point it out. (NY: E.P. Dutton, 1899.)

115 "'Alice in Wonderland', at the Opera Comique" This tear sheet from the issue of the 18th of January 1890 of *The Sketch* includes reproductions of photographs of Rose Hersee as Alice, Nesta de Becker as the Tiger Lily, and Phyllis Beadon as the Rose.

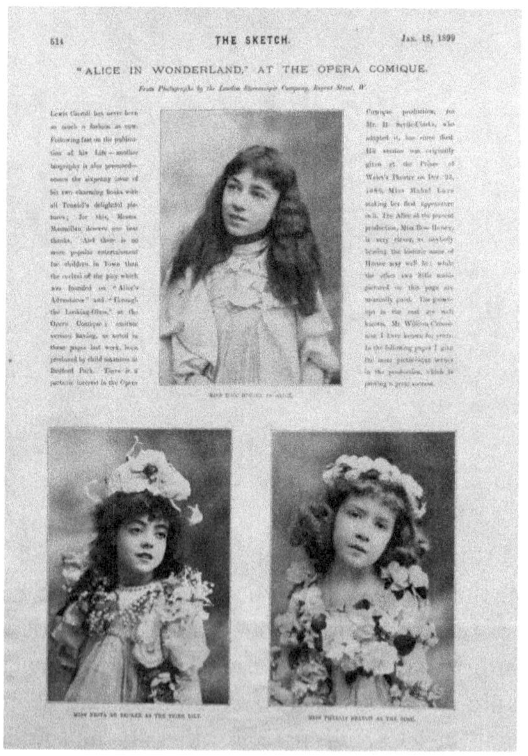

116–117 (116): The program exhibited here is from a performance of Savile Clarke's *Alice* at The Vaudeville Theatre in London that opened on December 19, 1900. An already famous adult actress, Ellaline Terriss, was given the lead role of Alice, and her husband, the actor Seymour Hicks, the role of the Hatter. This would not be the last time that a grown woman would star in the role of Alice, demanding a major stretch of belief from the audience. (117): This tear sheet, displaying illustrations for "Alice in Wonderland / A Dream Play for Children," is from the *Illustrated London News*, [ca. December 1900] about Savile Clarke's *Alice* performance at the Vaudeville Theatre, starring Ellaline Terris as Alice.

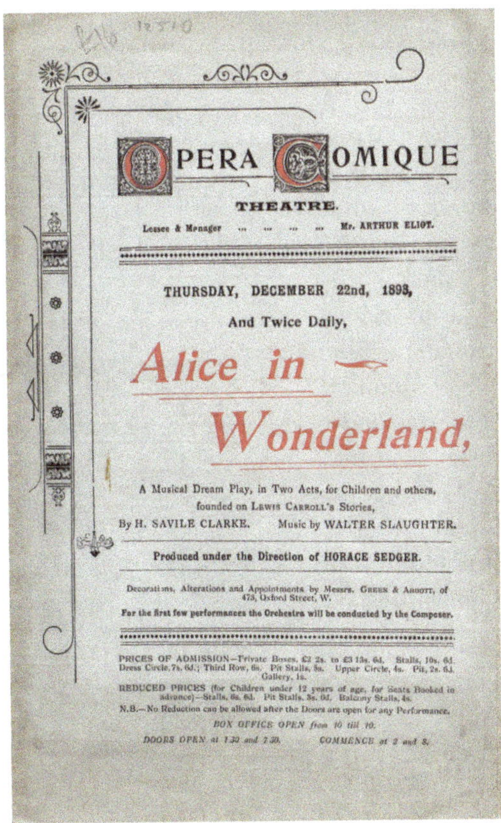

118: The exhibition also includes an Edwardian postcard signed by Ellaline Terris.

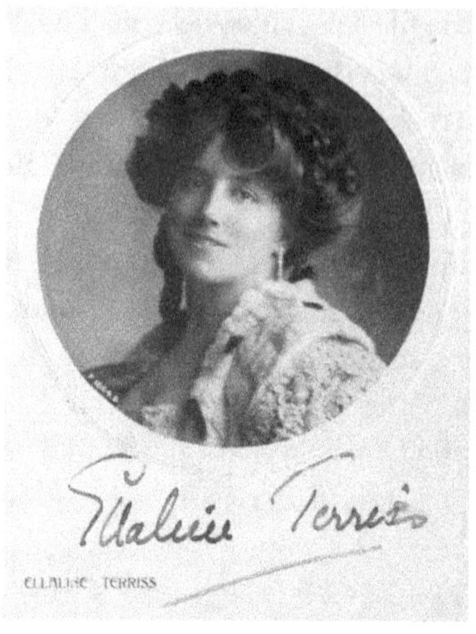

119–121 (119): Marie Studholme, another already famous adult actress, was chosen for the role of Alice in the 1906 revival of Savile Clarke's *Alice*. The issue of the 30th of January 1907 of *The Bystander* had an article about her, entitled "Alice Meets the White Rabbit / Miss Marie Studholme, in *Alice in Wonderland* at the *Prince of Wales*".

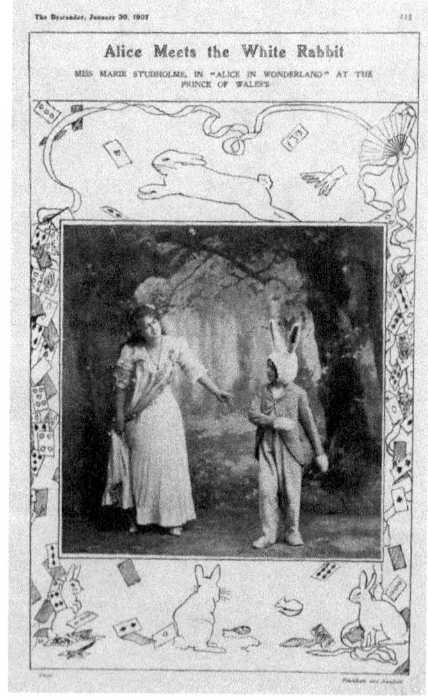

(120–121): Also exhibited here is a "Rotary Photographic postcard" (produced in huge multiples by rotary drum printers) depicting a costumed "Marie Studholme / as Alice in Wonderland".

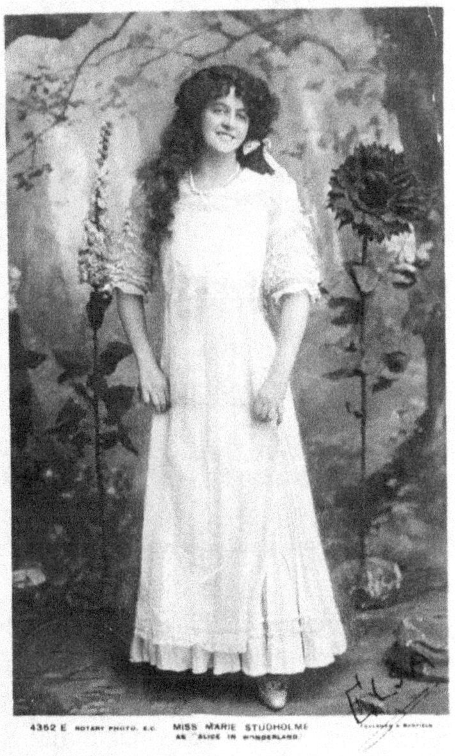

122–123 (122): Maidie Andrews, a beautiful Edwardian child actress who was closer to an appropriate age for a role as Alice, appeared in *Alice Through the Looking-Glass* at *The New Theatre* in 1903–04. This charming photograph of her in costume as Queen Alice appeared in *The Black and White Illustrated Budget* (a weekly newspaper) in 1904. (123): This 1905 "real photograph" postcard was inscribed by Andrews.

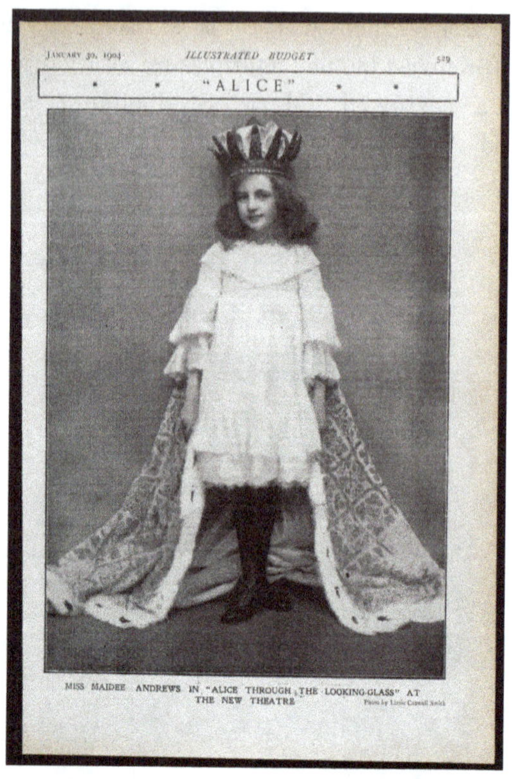

MISS MAIDEE ANDREWS IN "ALICE THROUGH THE LOOKING-GLASS" AT THE NEW THEATRE
Photo by Lizzie Caswall Smith

124 Irving Berlin, composer. This Edison "Blue Amberol" cylinder recording of "Alice in Wonderland" in its original cardboard sleeve is from the musical, *The Century Girl* (1916), and features a duet by Gladys Rice and Irving Kaufman. The title of this love song is the only Carrollian allusion.

125 "Eva Le Gallienne". This publicity photograph of Le Gallienne (1899–1991; English) was for her role in a 1925 theatrical performance of *The Call of Life*. She became a prominent American producer and director during the first half of the 20th century. Associated with her efforts she co-authored with actress Florida Friebus (1909–1988; American) a dramatization of *Alice* and *Looking-Glass* (*Alice in Wonderland*, NY, London and Los Angeles: Samuel French, 1932.) The

dramatization was frequently performed at Le Gallienne's own off-Broadway theatre (The Civic Repertory Theatre). A young Josephine Hutchinson had the lead role of Alice; Le Gallienne took the role of the White Queen.

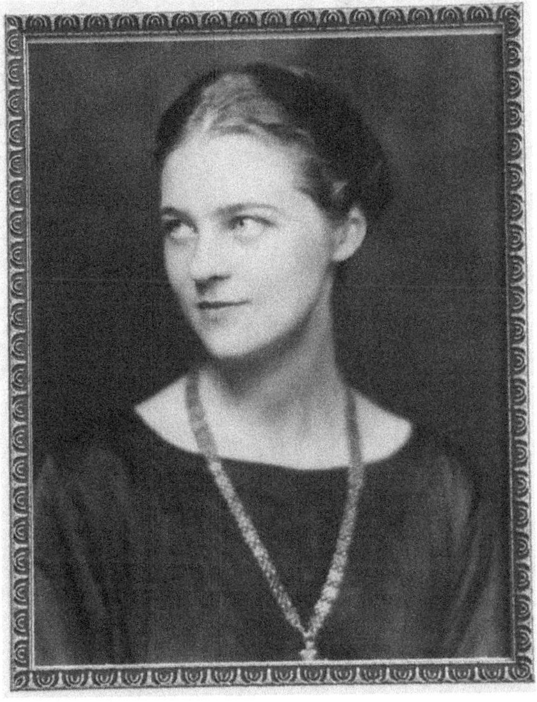

126 This publicity still, depicting Josephine Hutchinson in costume as Alice on-stage next to one of the sets, was purportedly from Eva Le Gallienne's personal archive and written on the back in her hand is the comment: "Again notice the accuracy of the Cross-hatching" along with a penciled date 1932. This is a reference to the elaborate sets and costumes that successfully mimicked the iconic cross-hatching of Tenniel's original engravings.

127 This program for The Civic Repertory Theatre for the weeks of the 16th to the 18th of January [1933] includes the cast members for six scheduled performances of *Alice*.

128 Eva Le Gallienne's dramatization of *Alice* was revived in 1947, starring the famed ballet dancer Bambi Linn (born Bambina Linnemeir) (1926–; American) in the role of Alice. Linn had made her Broadway debut in the original 1943 production of *Oklahoma!*

129 This souvenir program is from a performance of the 1947 revival. *Eva Le Gallienne / Margaret Webster and Bambi Linn / in Eva Le Gallienne's Production of / Alice in Wonderland / A Play with Music.*

130 This publicity still shows Bambi Linn in costume as Alice for the Le Gallienne 1947 revival of *Alice in Wonderland* at the Rita Hassan-American Repertory Theatre on the 31st of March 1947. This performance was broadcast on the weekly radio program, "House of Mystery", on Easter Sunday, the 6th of April 1947 on the Mutual Network, starring Eva Le Gallienne, Margaret Webster (1905–1972; American), and Bambi Linn.

131 Eva Le Gallienne' dramatization was revived again in 1983 with Kate Burton (daughter of Richard and Sybil Burton) (1957–; Swiss born Welsh-American) in the lead role as Alice. This poster by designer Bob Gill, featuring a Tenniel image of Alice opening up like a telescope, advertises the play at The Virginia Theatre in NYC.

132–133 (132): This copy of *The Playbill / For The Virginia Theatre*, Vol. 1, No. 4, Jan. 1983 is for the opening night performance of Le Gallienne's 1983 revival of *Alice in Wonderland*. It is signed by various members of the cast, including Eva Le Gallienne (White Queen), Kate Burton (Alice), Edward Hibbert (1955–; American; Gryphon), MacIntyre Dixon (1931–; American; Mad Hatter), and Geoff Garland (1932–2006; English; the Two of Spades). (133): In this publicity still Kate Burton, in costume as Alice, is holding a live pig-baby.

134 This wonderful advertising poster is for *Alice in Wonderland and Through the Looking Glass* performed by the Royal Shakespeare Company (RSC) at the Barbican Theatre in 2001. The performance was not well received by reviewers and closed early. It is considered a flop.

135 Shirley Temple (1928–2014; American), seen here costumed as Alice in Wonderland, is talking with actresses Esther Williams (1921–2013; American) and Janet Blair (1921–2007; American) during the "Photographer's Costume Ball" at Ciro's (a famous Hollywood night club) in 1948. Unfortunately, Temple never performed the role of Alice in a film.

136   This program is for The Charleston Ballet 1996–97 "Storybook Season" production of Yves de Bouteiller's *Alice in Wonderland*. Principal ballerina Kim Pauley danced the title role of Alice with Bouteiller himself dancing the role of the White Rabbit. The front wrap has been inscribed by seven members of the Company, including Pauley, Bouteiller, Angela Price (Caterpillar), Rita Green (Dormouse), Brooke Baker (Queen of Hearts), Rhiannon Lytton (March Hare), and Samuel Pergande (Mad Hatter).

137 *Alice's Adventures in Wonderland and Through the Looking-Glass.* Illustrated with photoplay scenes from the 1915 silent Nonpareil feature film starring Viola Savoy (1899–?; American) as Alice. (NY: Grosset and Dunlap, 1918.) Though this was a very early *Alice* film, it had been superseded by a 1903 UK film by Cecil Hepworth (1874–1953; English) and Percy London Stow (1876–1919; English), and by a 1910 silent film, directed by Edwin Stanton Porter (1870–1941; American).

138–139 (138): This publicity still is of Charlotte Henry (1914–1980; American), who starred in the 1933 *Alice* Paramount film. For the lead role of Alice, Paramount auditioned over 6,800 girls. The movie had an all-star cast (Cary Grant as the Mock Turtle; Gary Cooper as the White Knight; W. C. Fields as

Humpty Dumpty; etc.), but the heavy makeup and bulky costumes made it difficult to recognize them by anything except their familiar voices. (139): *Alice in Wonderland / The Story of the motion picture "Alice in Wonderland, a Paramount picture based upon the story by Lewis Carroll.* This "Big Little Book", No.759, is illustrated throughout with scenes from the 1933 Paramount film. (Racine, WI: Whitman Publishing Company, 1934.) (139A): This rare "jumbo" lobby card is from the 1933 Paramount film. Alice is shown here with Sterling Holloway, costumed as the Frog-footman. This specific image was used for the cover of the "Big Little Book" edition.

140   This rare double-page spread was pre-1951 concept publicity issued by Walt Disney for the contemplated animated version of *Alice*. This specific example appeared in *The American Weekly* insert in the *Chicago Herald-American* newspaper for August 11, 1946. One suspects that most people would agree that Disney's original vision was badly flawed.

141 Lou Bunin (1911–1994; American), a pioneering special effects innovator of stop-action films and a prominent puppeteer, made the mistake of producing a feature-length film version of *Alice* in 1949, shortly before the release of Walt Disney's 1951 animated *Alice*. A lawsuit from Walt Disney prevented it from being widely released in the U.S., so that it would not compete with Disney's forthcoming 1951 version. Carol Marsh (1926–2010; English) starred as Alice, even though she was 23 years old, perhaps because of her English accent and long blonde hair. She is the oldest woman to ever play the role of Alice in a film version.

142–143 (142): This BBC publicity still is a Mad Tea-Party scene from Jonathan Miller's (1934–; English) 1966 black and white made-for-TV film, starring a then unknown young girl, Anne-Marie Mallik (1952–; English) as Alice; sadly, she never made another film. The other actors at the table in this scene are comedians Peter Cook (1937–1995; English), Wilfred Lawson

(1900–66; English), and Michael Gough (1916–2011; English). Some Carrollians, including the compiler of this catalogue, regard this as the best (and funniest) cinema version of *Alice* ever produced. The cast of other luminaries, includes John Gielgud (1904–2000; English) as the Mock turtle, Peter Sellers (1925–80; British) as the King of Hearts, and Michael Redgrave (1908–2012; English) as the Caterpillar. Ravi Shankar (1920–2012; Bengali) wrote and performed the sitar music played throughout the film. The movie is biting satire about English society. Miller received mixed reviews, of course. Nonetheless, a feature review that appeared in *Vogue* for Dec. 1966 had this very positive opinion: "The subtle, lyrical, exact logic of the Wonderland child of Lewis Carroll has been netted. Again this unforgettable, one-hundred-and-one-year-old fantasy of childhood happens, this time through the poetic reasoned imagination of Jonathan Miller, who especially wrote, organized, and directed a new film of *Alice* to be shown on British television on New Year's Day. Holding to Carroll, dropping Tenniel, Dr. Miller changed the dreams to marvelously fresh and detailed Victoriana." (143): This splendid 1991 photograph of Jonathan Miller, director of the 1966 BBC version of *Alice*, was taken by *The Seattle Times* photographer Benjamin Benschneider. Miller has been many things in his life, including: a British theatre and opera director; actor; author; television presenter; humorist; sculptor; and, medical doctor.

144–145 (144): *Surrealistic Pillow*. This is the second album by American rock band *Jefferson Airplane*, and the first with vocalist Grace Slick, who sings "White Rabbit", a song which she wrote, with numerous allusions to *Alice*, and is an early example of psychedelic rock. (RCA Victor, LSP-3766 Stereo; first pressing, 1967.) (145): "Amazing Grace." This advertisement, from a January 1977 issue of *Playboy*, is for an upcoming interview with Grace Slick to be published in the February 1977 issue of *Oui*. By this time in her career Slick had left *Jefferson Airplane* for *Jefferson Starship*. This wonderful caricature, by an unidentified artist, shows Slick floating in a space suit tethered to a "musical note-shaped" starship, pointlessly playing a guitar (there is, of course, no sound in the vacuum of space). She is accompanied on the spacewalk by a space suited White Rabbit.

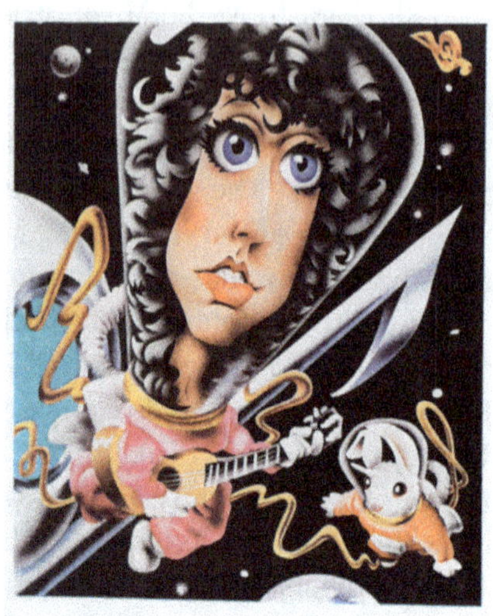

Amazing Grace

146–147 (146): This souvenir program for the 20th Century Fox 1972 movie version of *Alice* is inscribed or signed by nine cast members, including: Peter Sellers (1925–1980; British); Spike Milligan (1918–2000; India born, English/Irish); Dudley Moore (1935–2000; English); Roy Kinnear (1934–1988; British); Flora Robson (1902–1984; English); Ralph Richardson (1902–1983; English); Fiona Fullerton (1956–; Nigerian born, British; starring as Alice); Hywel Bennet (1944–; Welsh); and, Michael Crawford (1942–; English). This copy was reputedly signed at a cast party after completion of the film. The original owner supposedly traded it for a painting he liked; it must have been a great painting to have lost this program for! (147): This original 1972 lobby card for 20th Century Fox's *Alice* is a scene from "Pig and Pepper", with the Cook (played by Patsy Rowlands [1931–2005; English]), Alice (played by Fiona Fullerton), Duchess (Peter Bull [1912–1984; British]), and the baby (unidentified in the cast list). (147): This *"grande"*(47" x 63") one-sheet poster for *Alice au pays des Merveilles* [*AIW*] was released by Rossel Films in 1973. This is the French version of 20th Century Fox's 1972 film version of *Alice*.

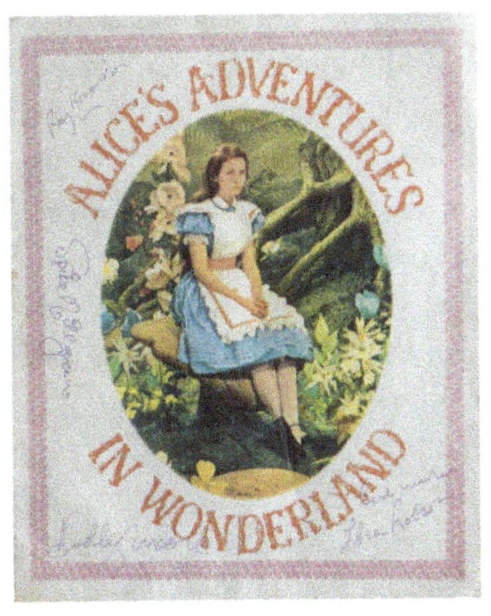

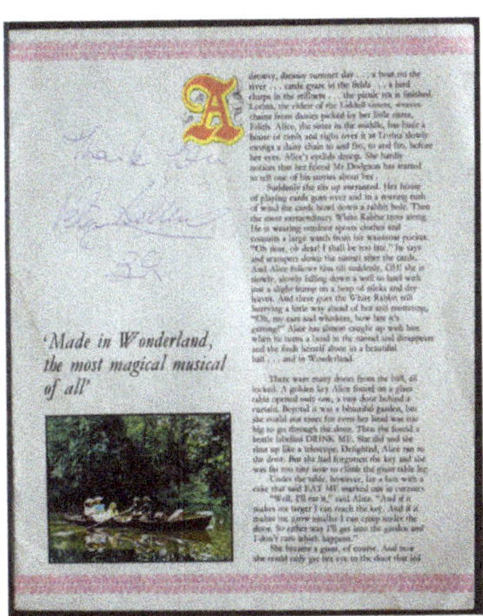

148   This one-sheet poster is for the German release of the 1977 British fantasy film, *Jabberwocky*, co-written and directed by Terry Gilliam (1940–; American) and starring Monty Python comedian Michael Palin (1943–; English).

149–150 (149): This elaborate promotional give-away for Tim Burton's (Walt Disney) 2010 film *Alice in Wonderland* was issued in 2009 to a limited number of influential film critics and reviewers. It was not for sale and difficult for a normal collector to obtain. It basically consists of three deluxe inter-stashed (book-in-a-book-in-a-book) faux books, with a key incorporating a USB device that allows viewing a preview of the film. (150): This is a cinema lobby display for Tim Burton's blockbuster 2010 film, *Alice in Wonderland*. A Disney sequel, *Alice in Wonderland: Through the Looking-Glass* is reportedly in preparation for a scheduled premiere in May 2016.

151 *ALICE (in Wonderland)*. This image is of a ballet dancer in costume as the White Rabbit. Septime Webre (Cuban-American), artistic director. Matthew Pierce, composer. Liz Vandal (1969–; French Canadian), costume designer. This poster is for the world premiere of The Washington Ballet's production at the Kennedy Center's Eisenhower Theater, April 11–15, 2012.

152–155 Four Carrollian caricatures by David Levine (1926–2009; American), a longtime illustrator for *The New York Review of Books*. These splendid caricatures are extracted from a copy of James Playsted Wood's, *The Snark Was a Boojum / A Life of Lewis Carroll* (NY: Pantheon Books, 1966.) They include: (152): Carroll on a theatrical toy horse; (153): Carroll smirking in a theatre audience; (154): Carroll toting his heavy photographic gear; and, (155): Carroll's most famous illustrator, Sir John Tenniel.

156 *Alice in Wonderland*. This 1947 print, published by "Art Told Tales", reproduces a painting by Ayres Houghtelling (1912–2006; American). It is remarkable in that the entire story of *Alice* can be traced, scene by scene in the correct order, starting in the upper left-hand corner. The original painting was sold at a Sotheby's NY auction in 2012. The presale estimate was $10,000–$15,000, but realized $53,125. This was originally painted for use as a double-page spread in a 1947 eition of *Collier's* magazine.

157 This limited edition (reproduction) poster by American artist Justin Hampton was originally created for a "Ween" concert on August 30, 2009 at Golden Gate Park in San Francisco. "Ween" is the name of an American rock band formed in 1984 by Aaron Freeman (born Gene Ween) and Mickey Melchiondo (born Dean Ween). This ghoulish image has maniacal Wonderland characters feasting on The Caterpillar.

158 "Alice in a Field of Flowers". This photographic print by Stephen Durrenberger is one of a series of five *Alice*-inspired images featuring his daughter as Alice. Durrenberger is a well-known West Virginia photographer.

159 "Alice in Blunderland." This John Tenniel political cartoon appeared in the British weekly Victorian magazine, *Punch, or the London Charivari*, for October 30, 1880. This is a complete single issue. A parody of "The Mock Turtle's Story," appears on p. 198. The accompanying full-page cartoon appears on p. 199, with Alice, the Gryphon and the Mock Turtle.

160 "The Red Queen and the White; or, Alice in Thunderland." This political cartoon, drawn in the style of John Tenniel by an unknown artist, appeared in *Punch* for July 18, 1891.

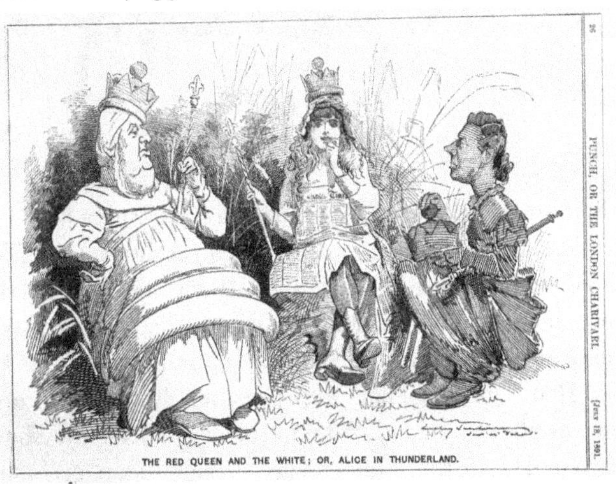

161   "Alice in Blunderland". This John Tenniel political cartoon concerning The Balfour Bill, starring the Gryphon and Mock Turtle, appeared in *Punch* in 1903. The Balfour Bill provided funds for religious instruction in voluntary elementary schools, owned primarily by the Church of England and Roman Catholics.

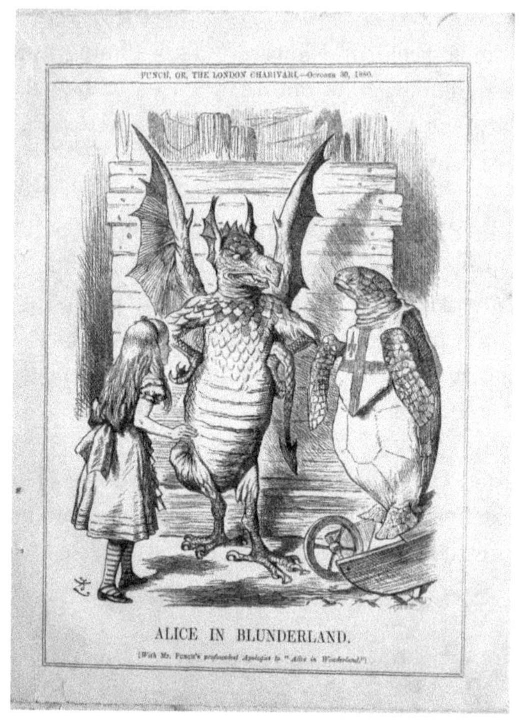

162   "Thinking Imperially". This Bernard Partridge (1861–1945; English) political cartoon (drawn in the style of John Tenniel) appeared in *Punch* for November 10, 1937. Adolf Hitler is lampooned as the White Queen. Queen Alice sits between him and his Italian counterpart, Benito Mussolini, who is lampooned as the Red Queen. They are presumably arguing amongst themselves about how to divide up the world after they have won World War II. All three queens are depicted as characters from *TTLG*. Partridge was named *Punch* Chief Cartoonist in 1910.

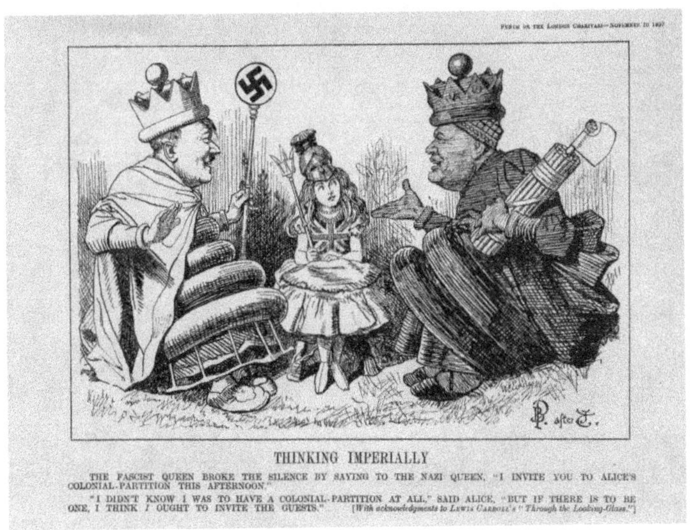

163 "Yet One More Conversation". This Bernard Partridge political cartoon (drawn in the style of John Tenniel) appeared in *Punch* for November 24, 1937. Adolf Hitler is lampooned as the Walrus and Lord Halifax (1881–1959; English) as the Carpenter, both from *TTLG*. Lord Halifax is more accurately named Edward Frederick Lindley Wood, 1st Earl of Halifax and as The Viscount Halifax from 1934 until 1944, the period in which this cartoon was published.

164 "Buddy Tucker and Alice of Wonderland, and Visit the Dog Who Worried the Cat [sic]." This is a tear sheet from a very early comic strip published in a Sunday newspaper comic section in the *New York Herald* in 1905, illustrated by R. F. Outcault (born Richard Felton Outcault) (1863–1928; American). This is quite fragile, due to oxidation of the cheap paper, and is quite rare. It's rather amazing that it has survived this long. These episodes were eventually published in 1907 by Cupples & Leon as *Alice in Wonderland Meets Buddy Tucker*, which has a notoriously fragile binding.

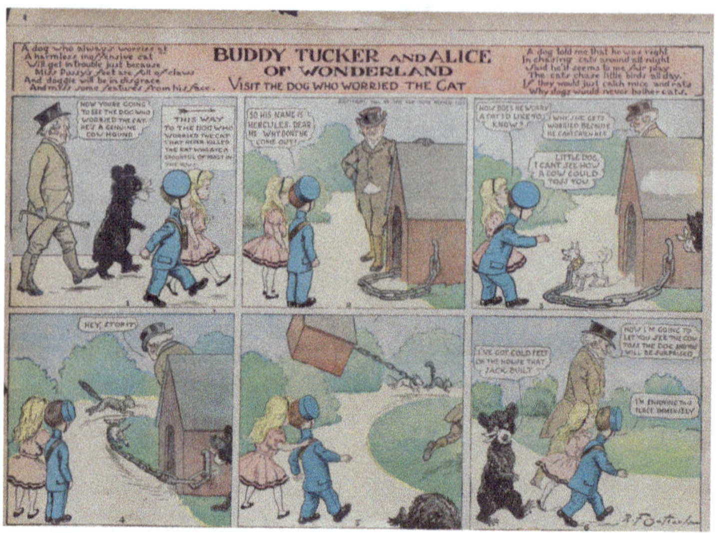

165 *"Alice in Wonderland / Illustrated Classic."* This is an original Sunday newspaper comic section illustrated by Alex Blum (born Alexander Anthony Blum) (1889–1969; Hungarian) and published in *The Chicago Sun* for July 13, 1947. These periodic strips were eventually collected and published in 1948 as No. 49 in the *Classics Illustrated* series of comic books by The Gilberton Company, an American publisher.

166 *Peanuts*. This tear sheet from *The Sun Journal* for the 15th of January 1977 is illustrated by Charles Shultz (born Charles Monroe Schultz) (1922–2000; American), featuring Snoopy performing his "Cheshire Beagle" trick. There were several comic strip episodes of Snoopy doing his exceptional dog trick.

167 "Lewis Carroll". This caricature of Lewis Carroll by David Levine (1926–2009; American) was first published in the *New York Review of Books* (*NYRB*) Vol. 26, No. 13, August 16, 1979. Shown here in this exhibition is a *NYRB* print of this image, which shows a dark, brooding and rather sinister Carroll with two young girls (child-friends) seated at his feet, undoubtedly an allusion to the fact that Levine disapproved of Dodgson's

interest in them and suspected the worst, even though there is no credible evidence that his relationships with any of them were anything inappropriate.

168–169 (168): "Through the Desk Drawers: or Alice's Adventures in the Political Wonderland." This original art for a political cartoon by James Dent (1928–1992; American) appeared in *The Charleston Gazette* (West Virginia) for November 5, 1984. Dent had a liberal political point of view. Former Republican Governor Arch Moore (1923–; American) is lampooned as the Mad Hatter. Moore was eventually convicted of corruption and served time in prison. Dent began work at *The Charleston Gazette* in 1952 and worked there until his death. The West Virginia Archives is now the repository for 5,700 of his political cartoons. The two in this exhibition managed to escape that fate when Dent gave them to Victoria Sewell for her collection. Arch Moore's daughter is United States Senator Shelly Moore Capito, newly elected for West Virginia. (169): "Alice's Adventures in West Virginia Wonderland." This original art for a political cartoon by James Dent appeared in *The Charleston Gazette* for September 11, 1990. Former Governor Arch Moore is again lampooned as the Hatter.

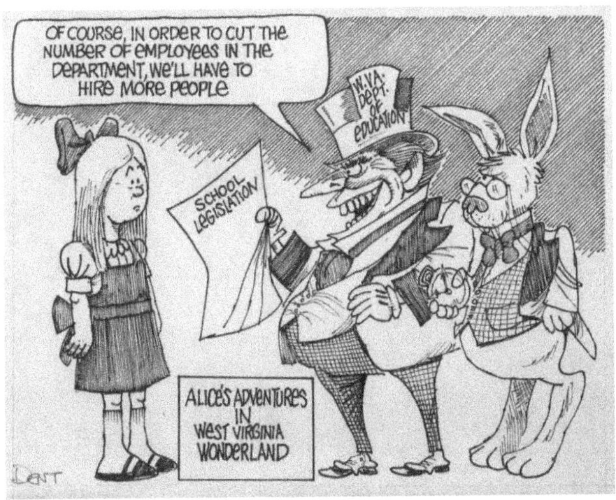

170–172 (170): *Alice*. This comic book-style book is illustrated by Lisa Dowling (ca. 1962–; American). According to the blurb, she has been a regular contributor to fantasy, sci-fi and comic art since 1976. She claims to be primarily influenced by Arthur Rackham and "Pogo" cartoons by Walt Kelly. (Thousand Oaks, CA: About Comics, 2004; first edition). (171): Original preliminary pencil sketch for page 38, signed by Lisa Dowling.

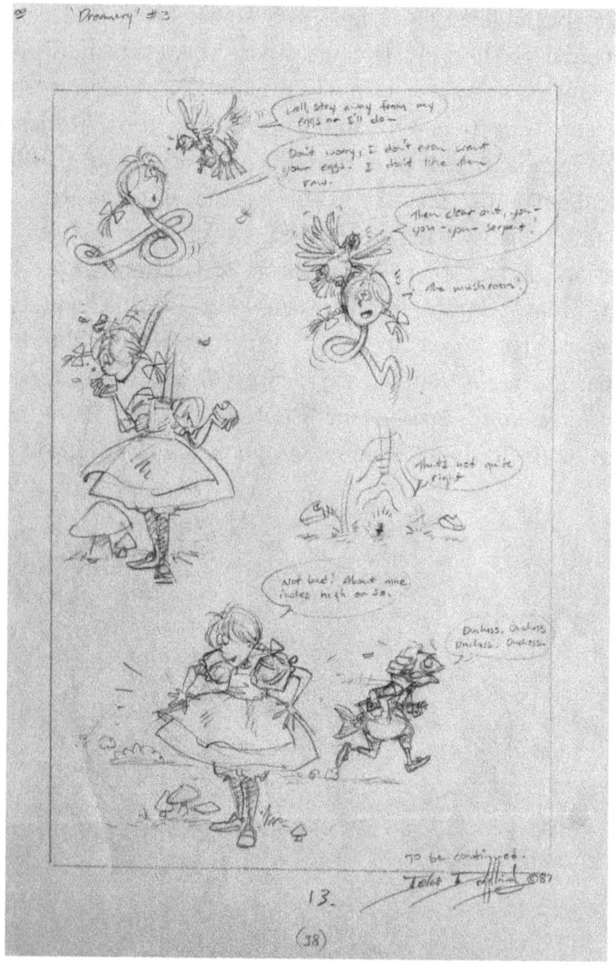

(172): Original final inked drawing for page 27, signed by Dowling. This has the original production overlay for the text affixed to the illustration board.

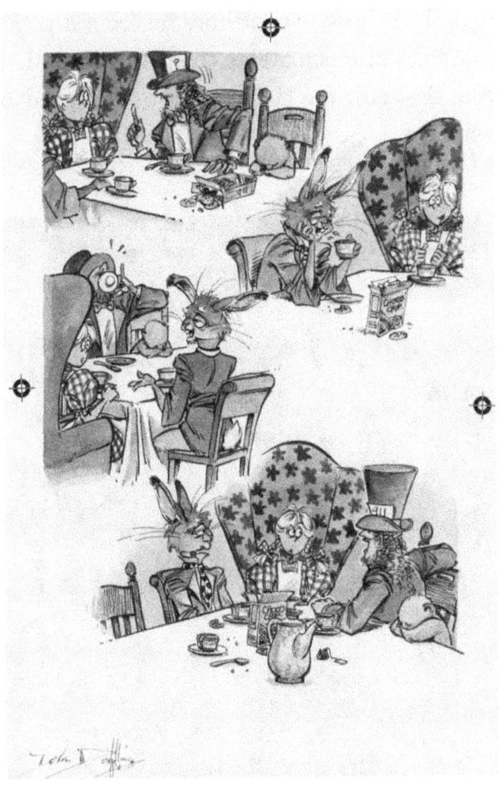

173 *Alice Eats Wonderland / An Irreverent Annotated Cookbook Adventure*. Co-authored by August A. Imholtz, Jr. and Alison Tannenbaum (1946–; American). Illustrated by A. E. K. Carr (now Ann E. Kelbe; 1977–; American). This satirical cookbook provides real recipes for preparing numerous dishes made from many of the characters in the *Alice* books, including such things as Spindled Oysters, Welsh Rabbit, Iguana Tamales, Roasted Beetle Grubs, and Turtle Soup, though some of the ingredients may be a bit difficult to obtain. Imholtz is a past-president of the Lewis Carroll Society of North America, humorist, author, and

Carroll collector. He and his wife's Carroll collection includes one of the world's largest collections of Carroll's works in Russian. Alison Tannenbaum is a prominent Carroll collector, poet, retired neurosurgeon, road-kill taxidermist, botanist, and gourmet cook. Put these two authors together and you get darkly humorous and eclectic books like this! (Carlisle, MA: Applewood Books, 2009; first edition; this copy is inscribed by both Imholtz and Tannenbaum.)

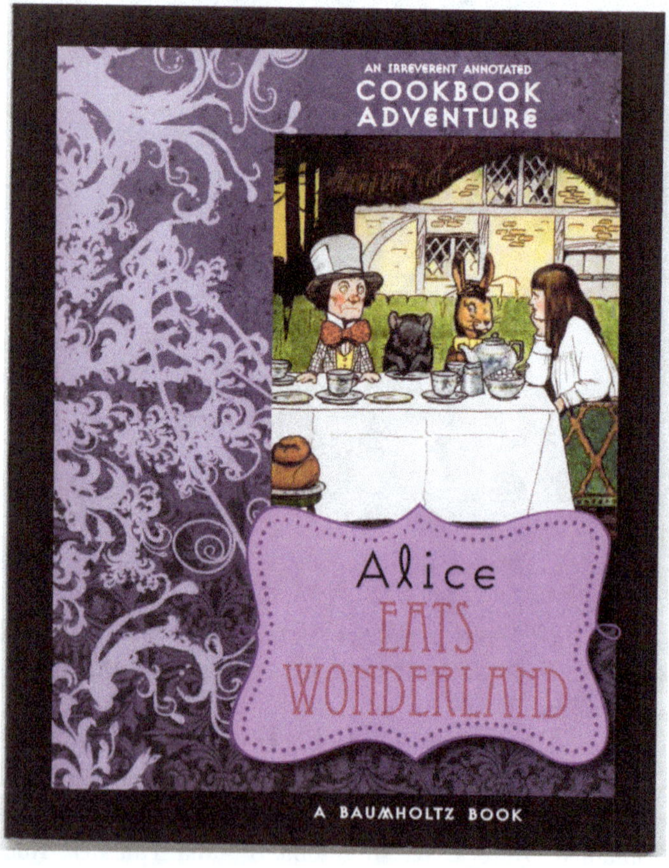

If this book appeals to you then you might also like another of their darkly humorous Carrollian works, *The Haunting of the*

Snarkasbord, a continuation of Carroll's classic nonsense poem, *The Hunting of the Snark*, which tells the grim fate of the crew. (Cathair na Mart: Evertype, 2012).

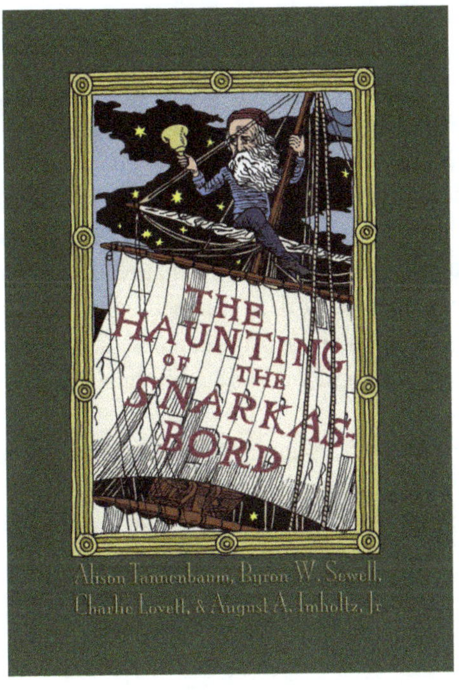

Selections from the Imholtz's vast personal Carroll collection will be exhibited at the University of Maryland's Hornbake Library (Aug. 2015–Aug. 2016) as a part of the Alice150 celebrations.

174   "Cheshire Cat". Original comic strip art by Dave Coverly (1964–; American). This panel was published July 22, 2011 as a daily *Speed Bump* cartoon. The original is inscribed and signed by Coverly.

175   "Alice in a Van Eyck Portrait". Jasmine Becket-Griffith (1979–; American) is a freelance artist specializing in fairy, fantasy and gothic art. She has created over thirty versions of *Alice,* including the print in this exhibition. The image is a parody

of the famous painting by Jan van Eyck (1394–ca. 1441; Flemish), entitled "Portrait of Giovanni Arnolfini and His Wife" (1434). In keeping with Becket-Griffith's gothic themed art, the husband is wearing a plague mask (a bird-like mask that doctors wore in an ineffective attempt to ward off infection by the Black Death), which doesn't bode well for either them or their child. Alice, who has taken the place of Giovanni's wife, is pregnant. Images of a pregnant Alice are, at the very least, uncommon. This is one of Becket-Griffith's better images, in contrast to many others, which can be cloyingly cute. One imagines that Carroll would not have been amused if he had lived to see this image. However, the same could be said for many modern images of Alice, especially in the modern *Alice*-themed comic books published by Zenescope, where she is often depicted as an overly-buxom, scantily clad adult engulfed in excessively bloody, horrific violence.

176 "Alice in a Box". Ginger Beth (née Sewell) Spath (1957–; American), artist. This 2013 humorous construction of found objects features Walt Disney's 1951 version of *AIW*.

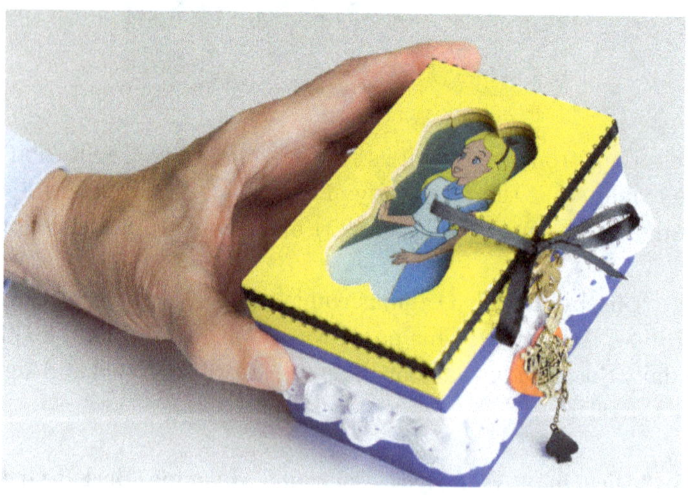

A small wooden box with a hinged lid has been painted to mimic Disney's version of Alice: the top of the lid is painted yellow

(Alice's straight hair); a black ribbon affixed to the rim around the lid (her hair band); a wide, white lace border (her pinafore); and, the box's sides painted blue (her dress).

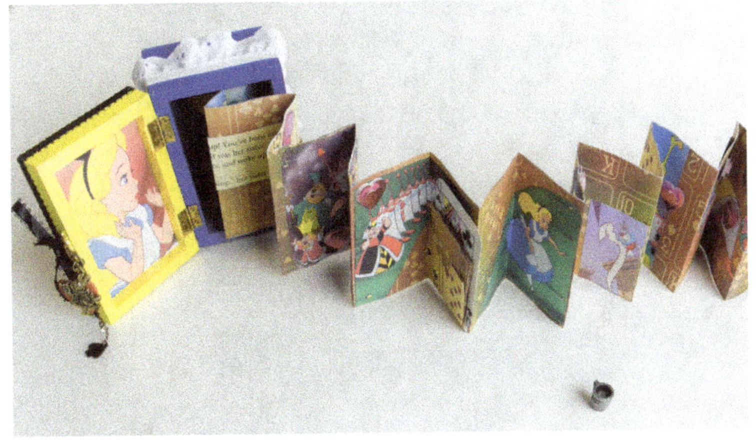

When the lid is opened a concertina-style foldout emerges (resembling a slow Jack-in-the-box). Both sides of the concertina are collaged with text and illustrations cut from a cheap Disney *Alice* edition acquired for a pittance at a garage sale. It tells the entire Disney version in proper sequence when read front to back. The small object in the foreground is a miniature Starbuck's coffee cup, which is included in the box.

177 "Stuck in Wonderland." Jett Jackson (born Laura Lee Jackson) (1958–; American). This is a commercially produced print of a painting by Jackson, who has done a number of *Alice*-inspired works and this iconic image, in which a tattooed Alice is waiting tables in a Wonderland café, is one of her best. Her paintings are often simultaneously surreal, charming, humorous, and poignant. If you, like many people, are fascinated by this particular image of *Alice* then please see Andrew Sellon's review of the painting, reprinted near the end of this catalogue. (The *Knight Letter*, the Lewis Carroll Society of North

America's official magazine, Volume II, Issue 11, No. 81, pp. 17–18).

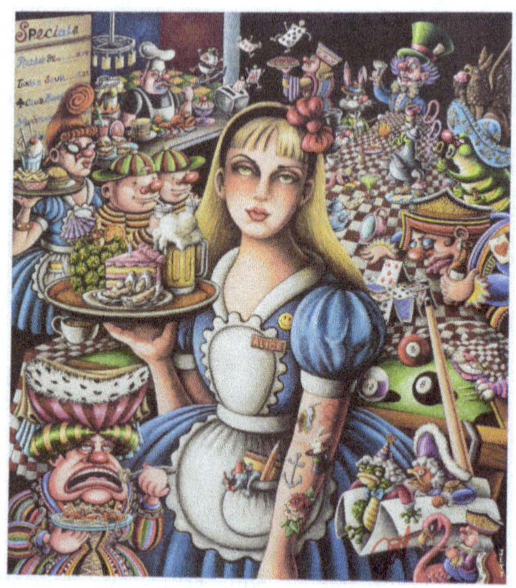

178   This ca. 1900–1910 American doll, by an unknown manufacturer, has the original costume as Alice. She has a bisque face and cloth body. The doll was collected in an antique shop in Lewisburg, WV. This photograph shows her on a bench, decorated by a West Virginian craftsperson (ca. 2005) in an American primitive-style.

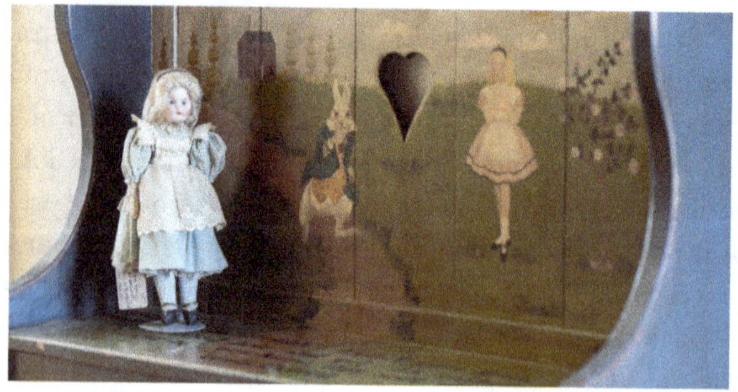

179 This ca. 1940–50 American doll, by an unknown manufacturer, has a plastic body and movable eyelids.

180 This ca. 1950–60 American doll was manufactured by Milton Bradley for a collection entitled "The StoryBook World of Bradley". She is in her original costume and has the original tag, which includes a very brief retelling of *Alice*. No. SD-478.

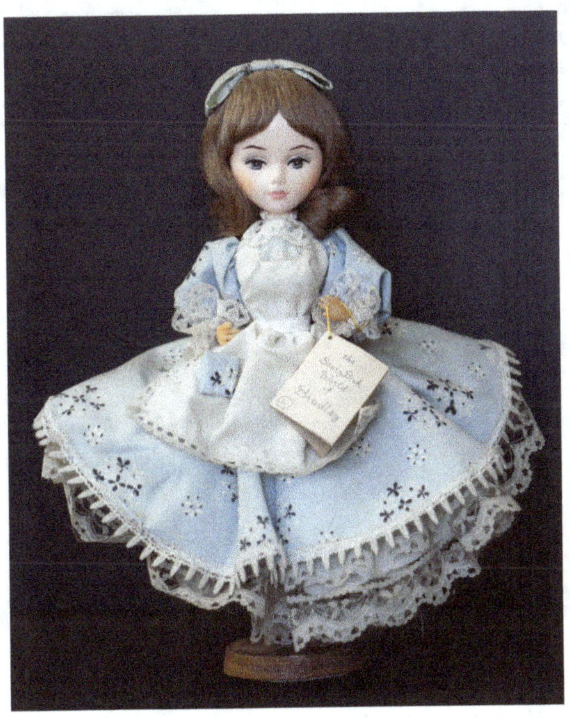

181 "Cream of Wheat". Illustrated after John Tenniel by an unidentified artist. Alice ladles Cream of Wheat into the cereal bowls of the Wonderland and Looking-Glass creatures assembled round the table at a "Mad Breakfast". According to Jessie Lasorda of the Mid-Michigan Genealogical Society (Lansing, MI), the model for "Rastus", the smiling Black-American chef in the Cream of Wheat ads, was Frank L. White

(1867–1938; Barbados-born, American). (*Ladies Home Journal*, August 1901).

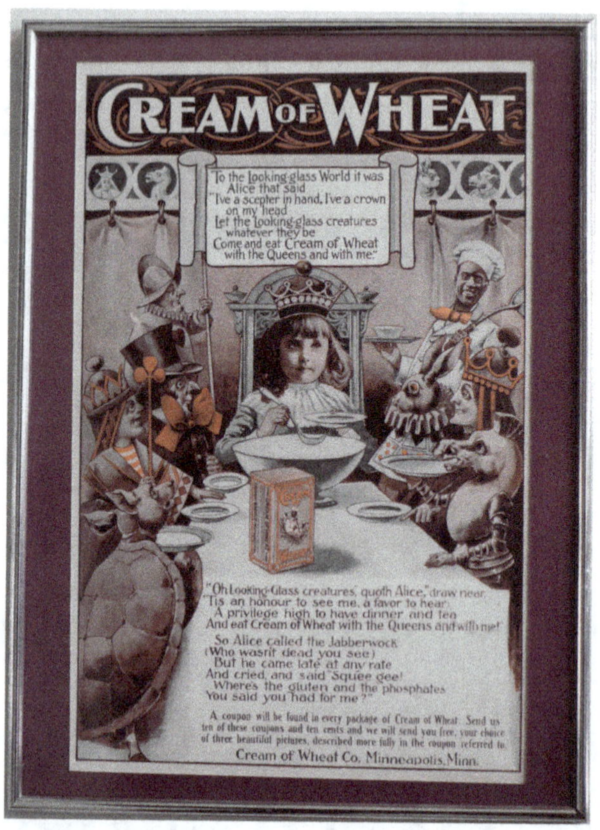

182 *The Harp of a Thousand Strings or Laughter for a Lifetime.* Samuel P. Avery, editor and engraver. This humor anthology, which was one of the most popular collections in 19th-century America, includes "Novelty and Romancement / A Broken Spell". It is the first appearance of any of Dodgson's work in a book and also the first reprinting anywhere of any of his works. This short piece first appeared in the monthly magazine *The Train* for March 1856, with only one illustration. In this appearance there are three illustrations. The publication was unauthorized by Dodgson and he was not attributed. The humor

concerns a shop's broken signboard advertising "Roman cement", hence the "broken spell[ing]". Most people would probably agree that Dodgson's humor improved dramatically with the appearance of *Alice*. (NY: Dick & Fitzgerald, 1858. First edition.)

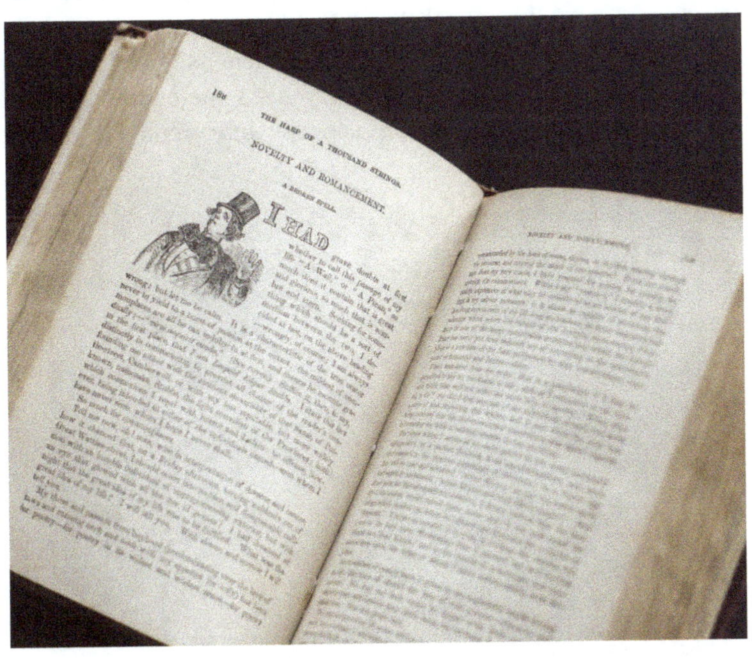

183 "Wanda Petunia as Alice in Wonderland". This plush toy was handcrafted in 2015 by Amy Jane Williams (1964–; American, West Virginia resident), therapist, conceptual street artist and author. In Williams' own words: "Porcine adventurer Wanda Petunia is an archetypal soul mate of Alice. Inquisitive, impulsive and irreverent… Wanda Petunia embodies creatively living and problem solving in the spirit of Alice. Had Wanda been born 150 years ago, she may well have joined Alice in her adventures. In the space-time continuum, she is happy to be with her now… helping children and adults find wonder again." You can visit http://amywilliamswellness.com to check out more about Amy and Wanda.

184 "Alice". Byron Sewell's etching/engraving was pulled in 1974 as a class assignment while studying print making at the University of Texas at Austin. The image is after Julia Margaret Cameron's ca. 1872 photograph of an adult Alice Liddell, costumed as Pomona, a nymph and the Roman goddess of fruit and gardens, famous for her chastity. Dodgson, Cameron's contemporary, strongly disliked her blurry, soft focus photographic style, even describing some of them as "hideous". That assessment is not shared with everyone, some of whom regard them as more painterly in concept and realization than Dodgson's.

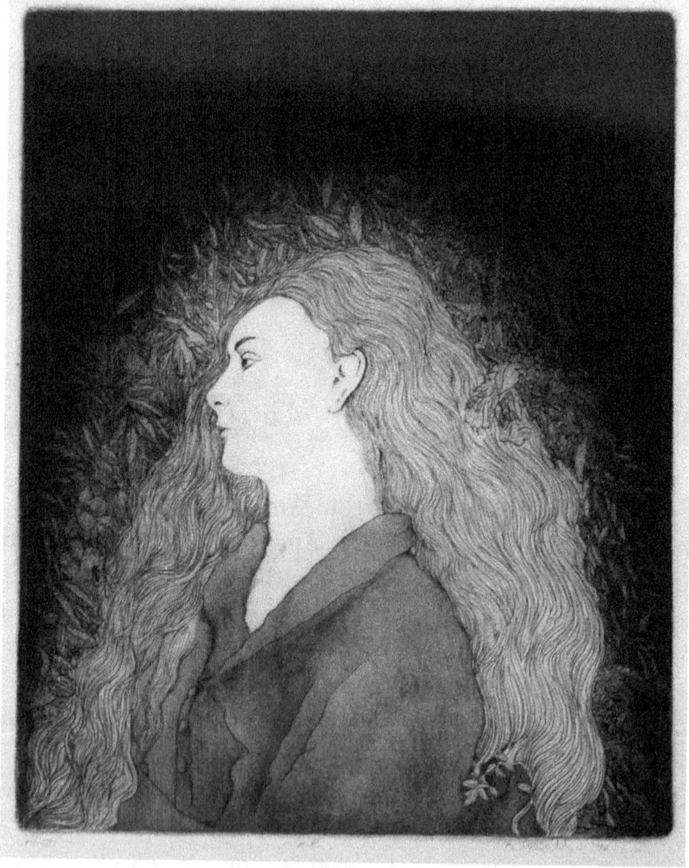

Jett Jackson's
Stuck in Wonderland

ANDREW SELLON
PRESIDENT EMERITUS,
LEWIS CARROLL SOCIETY OF NORTH AMERICA

Even those who have (gasp) never actually read *Alice's Adventures in Wonderland* and its sequel have probably seen one or more adaptations in one medium or another, and know that, in the end, Alice triumphs over the Queens and escapes the ever-madder realms of Wonderland and Looking-Glass Land for a presumably saner world. But what if Alice *hadn't* gotten out? That is the simple yet amusingly provocative premise behind artist Jett Jackson's latest *Alice*-themed artwork, *Stuck in Wonderland*, and to my eye there is a difference in tone worth noting in this latest creation, in comparison with her earlier *Alice* projects.

In a number of previous works, Jackson has depicted Alice as an aloof, sexually mature young woman with voluptuous golden curls and a penchant for revealing a bit of bosom—in other words, an Alice the original author would never have presented, and one more likely to provoke than please Carroll "traditionalists." In *Stuck*, however, Jackson finds a delightful middle ground and mines it to great effect. Here, Alice's Disney-blonde hair hangs down utterly straight—in simplicity, defeat, or perhaps both. And her trademark white pinafore is rendered for humor and irony, not sexual provocation, because this time, that archetypal garment has subtly morphed into a waitress's uniform. And while in some of Jackson's previous works Alice seemed to exert some measure of control, in this latest work, Alice is exactly what the title says: *stuck*.

The familiar Wonderland and Looking-Glass Land characters surround her, carrying on what appears to be a particularly out-of-control un-birthday party, while Alice stands center, looking away from it all. Her expression is inscrutable—as it is in previous Jackson works, and arguably as it is in Tenniel's original images—but this time there seems to be a hint of bittersweet dreaming behind the blankness. While the revelers cavort red-nosed around her, Alice looks out almost at us, almost a latter-day Mona Lisa. Is she dreaming of being back under the tree, wide awake, while her older sister reads a pictureless history book, or of posing for Mr. Dodgson's photographs in his rooms at Oxford, or perhaps just of resting her aching dogs on an old ottoman in a tiny East Village studio? Jackson playfully invites us to speculate. And while we're with Alice in this "No Exit" Wonderland Diner, Jackson also invites us to take a long, detailed look at the dive in which our heroine finds herself marooned.

Given the number of tattoos on her arm (this is still not a purist's Alice), one has the feeling that poor Alice has been there for quite some time. Her inkings range from story-related (a white rabbit, a white rose half-painted red) to surreal homage (a melting Dali watch). And Alice's customers? Evidently it's always beer time here. The Queen of Hearts is out cold, head on the table, still clutching a bottle. The similarly incapacitated dormouse, replete with his own tiny bottle and a mysterious little fez, hangs draped out of Alice's apron pocket. The Tweedles are literally cross-eyed, and most of the other characters are doing their best to catch up.

Only a few of the many creatures crowded into the diner still have their wits about them: the Duchess is busily wolfing down a huge plate of spaghetti, a second waitress in 1950s glasses efficiently plows through the addled crowd with her tray, and the short-order cook is making a lobster dish with one hand while tossing a Humpty omelette with the other. Part of the fun of this work is scanning it for the thematic visual jokes tucked here and there (check out the Specials board and the items on Alice's tray, for example).

In the midst of all the madness, large as life and twice as detached, stands our heroine, with her crisp uniform, "Alice" name tag, and smiley-face button. Just as Carroll did with his original stories, Jackson gives us an Alice who is a stranger in a strange land, performing tasks that are beneath her with some measure of grace, in a world crammed with creatures behaving badly—in other words, someone with whom we can all identify. But even if this Alice hasn't yet found the exit, Jackson seems to be giving us a tiny bit of hope that one day she may.

INTERVIEW WITH ARTIST JETT JACKSON

After writing about the work *Stuck in Wonderland,* I interviewed artist Jett Jackson to hear her take on it and on her history of *Alice* projects. Ms. Jackson is an extremely amiable conversationalist, eager to discuss what she puts into her work, and what others think of it. She estimated that she has created around a thousand paintings so far in her career. She noted that in general, she tends to fill her works with references to world art history, love, melancholy, and humor, with a slight nod to cartoons. Surrealism is a favorite device, although she does not consider herself a surrealist in the strict sense. She explained that a number of the image choices in *Stuck,* including some characters, occur in some of her earlier works, and as a result, her pieces tend to contain something of a personal art history as well.

Despite an avowed openness to the sensual side of life, she stated that she is surprised when viewers sometimes "over-sexualize" her *Alice* images. Yet at the same time, she acknowledged a joy in tweaking or provoking her audience. In one of her Carroll-themed works, *Alice at the Barbeque*, Alice is grilling the white rabbit—literally. Not all of Jackson's *Alice* images are that extreme, but she did note that her series has strong themes of the heroine seizing control over an unfair world, and even meting out a diva's revenge in some cases. When asked where her ideas for a new piece come from, Jackson said she felt that "The more I put myself out on a limb personally, the more people would be likely to connect with it." But Jackson readily agreed that while *Stuck* still has wild elements, its message is gentler. She said she reworked Alice's face many times to find the right balance in the expression.

Jackson noted with amusement that she herself has long blond hair and blue eyes, and that comparisons to Alice are inevitable, if not necessarily accurate. She is only too aware of all the *Alice*-loving artists and readers out there: "I was extremely conscious of the fact that there would be an audience very knowledgeable of the original illustrations. And I wanted to honor those images, as I loved them too! I like bringing *Alice* into the modern world."

Alice150 Celebrations and Exhibitions

*N*ote: Be sure to verify location and dates before planning to attend any of these venues, since dates and times for some are unknown at this writing and may change without notice.

On October 9–11 of 2015 the LCSNA will hold a conference at Lincoln Center campus auditorium of the **New York Institute of Technology** and **New York University**, which will focus on *"Alice in the popular culture"*.

Columbia University will mount an exhibit with memorabilia from their 1932 celebration of the centennial of Carroll's birth; Mrs. Hargreaves was in attendance.

New York University, which holds the extensive Alfred C. Berol Collection of Carroll material, will mount an exhibit of *Alice* parodies and ephemera.

The Morgan Library, which will feature important Lewis Carroll and *Alice* material from their own collection in an exhibit running June through October 11, 2015. The British Library will lend Carroll's original manuscript of *Alice's Adventures under Ground* to The Morgan during this time.

The New York Public Library for the Performing Arts (LPA) will mount an exhibit of "*Alice* in Performance" in the Vincent Astor Gallery. The exhibition will be selected from their dance, theater, and music archives, as well as a private collection. In conjunction there will be screenings of historically important *Alice* films.

The USBBY (the United States chapter of **The International Board on Books for Young People [IBBY]** will hold their 2015 Regional Conference in New York City, October 16–18, to coincide with Alice150.

The Grolier Club will mount an exhibit of Alice in translation, "Alice in a World of Wonderlands." A vast assortment of translated books and ephemera will be on display.

A **three-day colloquium** on translations with an international array of translators and scholars will be held on Tuesday – Thursday, October 6–8 at The Grolier Club. Reservations are required.

IN OTHER CITIES

In **Philadelphia**, the **Rosenbach Museum and Library** will display the *Under Ground* manuscript after the Morgan, which will signal a kick-off to city-wide events starting in October 2015, including four exhibitions: Maurice Sendak and Carroll, the anniversary and legacy of *Alice*, the Rosenbach and *Alice* (the ms., and Alice herself in Philadelphia), and a gaming room based on Dodgson's games and puzzles.

The Houghton Library's Modern Books and Manuscripts collection at **Harvard University** in **Cambridge** will hold a major exhibition.

The University of Maryland will hold a Carroll exhibition from August 2015 to August 2016.

The **Vassar College Library** in Poughkeepsie, NY, is planning an exhibition titled "The Age of Alice: Fantasy, Fairy Tales, and Nonsense in Victorian England" from the 28th of January through the 26th of May 2015

The Book Club of California will exhibit fine-press Carrollian works from May to August 2015.

The Lewis Carroll Society of North America

All Alice150 exhibitions and events in the USA are under the auspices of the Lewis Carroll Society of North America (LCSNA).

The LCSNA, founded in 1974, is an organization of Carroll admirers of all ages and interests, as well as a virtual center for Carroll studies. The Society has members throughout the world, including Australia, Brazil, Canada, Germany, Israel, Japan, The Netherlands, Russia, Sweden, the UK, with interests in virtually all of Lewis Carroll's many pursuits and in his continuing impact on our current culture.

While LCSNA meetings are free and open to the public, annual membership in the LCSNA has its privileges. Membership includes a free subscription to the Society's superb magazine, the *Knight Letter*, and a free copy of any member premium they produce during the current membership year. U.S. members also receive free shipping of the LCSNA publications. All members receive special rates on hotels for meetings (when available), advance notification of all upcoming events, and an exclusive membership pin.

You can contact the LCSNA on-line and sign up for membership at:

http://www.lewiscarroll.org/membership/

Acknowledgements

This catalogue is indebted to numerous annotations in Charlie Lovett's, *Alice 125 / 1865–1990 / Being a Checklist of 125 Landmark Publications in the History of Lewis Carroll's Alice in Wonderland*, (Winston-Salem, NC: privately printed, 1990) that have been adapted and/or quoted with the gracious permission of Charlie Lovett.

Edward Wakeling has kindly provided support and expertise in the preparation of some of the annotations in this catalogue.

The Sewells are grateful to Satish Bodepu (1984–; India) for graciously taking and processing all of the photographs appearing in this catalogue without remuneration.

All items in this exhibition are from the Lewis Carroll Collection of Victoria J. Sewell.

Alis'z Advenčrz in Wundrland,
Alice printed in the Ñspel orthography, 2015

[Nyctographic Square Alphabet text], *Alice* printed in the Nyctographic Square Alphabet, 2011

[Shaw Alphabet text], *Alice* printed in the Shaw Alphabet, 2013

ALISIZ ADVENCƎRZ IN WUNDRLAND,
Alice printed in the Unifon Alphabet, 2014

Behind the Looking-Glass: Reflections on the Myth of
Lewis Carroll, by Sherry L. Ackerman, 2012

Clara in Blunderland, by Caroline Lewis, 2010

Lost in Blunderland: The further adventures of Clara,
by Caroline Lewis, 2010

John Bull's Adventures in the Fiscal Wonderland,
by Charles Geake, 2010

The Westminster Alice, by H. H. Munro (Saki), 2010

Alice in Blunderland: An Iridescent Dream,
by John Kendrick Bangs, 2010

Rollo in Emblemland, by J. K. Bangs & C. R. Macauley, 2010

Gladys in Grammarland, by Audrey Mayhew Allen, 2010

Alice's Adventures in Pictureland,
by Florence Adèle Evans, 2011

Eileen's Adventures in Wordland, by Zillah K. Macdonald, 2010

Phyllis in Piskie-land, by J. Henry Harris, 2012

Alice in Beeland, by Lillian Elizabeth Roy, 2012

The Admiral's Caravan, by Charles Edward Carryl, 2010

Davy and the Goblin, by Charles Edward Carryl, 2010

*Alix's Adventures in Wonderland:
Lewis Carroll's Nightmare*, by Byron W. Sewell, 2011

Álobk's Adventures in Goatland, by Byron W. Sewell, 2011

Alice's Bad Hair Day in Wonderland,
by Byron W. Sewell, 2012

The Carrollian Tales of Inspector Spectre,
by Byron W. Sewell, 2011

Alice's Adventures in An Appalachian Wonderland,
Alice in Appalachian English, 2012

Alice tu Vãsilia ti Ciudii, *Alice* in Aromanian, 2015

Алесіны прыгоды ў Цудазем'і, *Alice* in Belarusian, 2013

Ahlice's Aveenturs in Wunderlaant,
Alice in Border Scots, 2015

Alice's Mishanters in e Land o Farlies,
Alice in Caithness Scots, 2014

Crystal's Adventures in A Cockney Wonderland,
Alice in Cockney Rhyming Slang, 2015

Aventurs Alys in Pow an Anethow, *Alice* in Cornish, 2015

Alice's Ventures in Wunderland, *Alice* in Cornu-English, 2015

Alices Hændelser i Vidunderlandet, *Alice* in Danish, 2015

La Aventuroj de Alicio en Mirlando,
Alice in Esperanto, by E. L. Kearney, 2009

La Aventuroj de Alico en Mirlando,
Alice in Esperanto, by Donald Broadribb, 2012

Trans la Spegulo kaj kion Alico trovis tie,
Looking-Glass in Esperanto, by Donald Broadribb, 2012

Les Aventures d'Alice au pays des merveilles,
Alice in French, 2010

Alice's Abenteuer im Wunderland, *Alice* in German, 2010

Alice's Adventirs in Wunnerlaun,
Alice in Glaswegian Scots, 2014

Balþos Gadedeis Aþalhaidais in Sildaleikalanda,
Alice in Gothic, 2015

Nā Hana Kupanaha a ʻĀleka ma ka ʻĀina Kamahaʻo,
Alice in Hawaiian, 2012

Ma Loko o ke Aniani Kū a me ka Mea i Loaʻa iā ʻĀleka ma
Laila, *Looking-Glass* in Hawaiian, 2012

Aliz kalandjai Csodaországban, *Alice* in Hungarian, 2013

Eachtraí Eilíse i dTír na nIontas,
Alice in Irish, by Nicholas Williams, 2007

Lastall den Scáthán agus a bhFuair Eilís Ann Roimpi,
Looking-Glass in Irish, by Nicholas Williams, 2009

Eachtra Eibhlís i dTír na nIontas,
Alice in Irish, by Pádraig Ó Cadhla, 2015

Le Avventure di Alice nel Paese delle Meraviglie,
Alice in Italian, 2010

L's Aventuthes d'Alice en Êmèrvil'lie, *Alice* in Jèrriais, 2012

L'Travèrs du Mitheux et chein qu'Alice y dêmuchit,
Looking-Glass in Jèrriais, 2012

Ia Aventures as Alice in Daumsenland,
Alice in Sambahsa, 2013

ʻO Tāfaoga a ʻĀlise i le Nuʻu o Mea Ofoofogia,
Alice in Samoan, 2013

Eachdraidh Ealasaid ann an Tìr nan Iongantas,
Alice in Scottish Gaelic, 2012

Alice's Adventirs in Wonderlaand, *Alice* in Shetland Scots, 2012

Alice Munyika Yamashiripiti, *Alice* in Shona, 2015

Ailice's Aventurs in Wunnerland,
Alice in Southeast Central Scots, 2011

Alices Äventyr i Sagolandet, *Alice* in Swedish, 2010

Ailis's Anterins i the Laun o Ferlies,
Alice in Synthetic Scots, 2013

ʻAlisi ʻi he Fonua ʻo e Fakaofoʻ, *Alice* in Tongan, 2014

Alice's Carрànts in Wunnerlan, *Alice* in Ulster Scots, 2013

Der Alice ihre Obmteier im Wunderlaund,
Alice in Viennese German, 2012

Ventürs jiela Lälid in Stunalän, *Alice* in Volapük, 2015

Lès-avirètes da Alice ô payis dès mèrvèyes,
Alice in Walloon, 2012

Anturiaethau Alys yng Ngwlad Hud, *Alice* in Welsh, 2010

Alison's Jants in Ferlieland, *Alice* in West-Central Scots, 2014

Di Avantures fun Alis in Vunderland, *Alice* in Yiddish, 2015

U-Alice Ezweni Lezimanga, *Alice* in Zulu, 2014

www.ingramcontent.com/pod-product-compliance
Lightning Source LLC
Chambersburg PA
CBHW060946050726
47592CB00003B/1128